BASIL FELDMAN

BASIL FELDMAN

MEMOIRS

LORD FELDMAN

Biteback Publishing

First published in Great Britain in 2014 by
Biteback Publishing Ltd
Westminster Tower
3 Albert Embankment
London SE1 7SP

ISBN 978-1-84954-761-1

10 9 8 7 6 5 4 3 2 1

A CIP catalogue record for this book is available from the British Library.

Set in Adobe Caslon Pro by Namkwan Cho

Printed and bound in Great Britain by
CPI Group (UK) Ltd, Croydon CR0 4YY

MIX
Paper from
responsible sources
FSC
www.fsc.org   FSC® C020471

This book is for Gita, with all my love

CONTENTS

FOREWORD

BY LORD SHERBOURNE

I first got to know Basil when I started working for Mrs Thatcher at No. 10 in 1983. Mrs Thatcher always admired people with a business background who had energy and 'get-up-and-go' and Basil had all of that, and more, in spades. He was fizzing with ideas and energy. Above all, he was a natural campaigner.

He was the inspiration and driving force behind the 'Better Made in Britain' campaign to boost the UK's manufacturing industry by encouraging the best in Britain to be made and bought. It was a great campaign.

Then Basil threw his energy behind the campaign to allow Sunday opening of stores – a policy that the Thatcher Government wanted to introduce, but against which there was fierce opposition. Basil, with his characteristic drive, pulled together a hugely impressive alliance of retailers and others. At this stage, I had left No. 10 and was part of the public relations team working on the campaign. Eventually the law was changed to liberalise shopping hours on Sundays and I believe that, but for Basil, it might never have happened.

But my abiding memories of Basil – whether working for the

Conservative Party, for one of his campaigns, or for one of his many charities – are ones of fun, energy and commitment. Basil knew everybody that mattered, and he got them on side.

I would call his career 'The irresistible rise of Basil Feldman and, above all, of the causes he held dear.'

Stephen Sherbourne
JULY 2014

INTRODUCTION

Why write a book like this one? Well, the first nudge was from my elder son Nick, who pointed out that my long life has not been uneventful.

I have lived during many of the most important changes in the twentieth century: the Second World War, the establishment of Israel as a country, the fall of the British Empire, the advent of television, the mobile phone, the internet ... I am of course not unique, but what might make my years more memorable than some is that I have come into contact with so many interesting and powerful people from all over the world. I am fortunate to have also been able to make my own contribution to change and progress. I have always had a social conscience, as well as a great deal of energy.

My parents met each other in London at the beginning of the twentieth century and remained grateful to the country which gave them their nationality, allowed them to settle here and make a life for themselves and their children. I have, of course, encountered anti-Semitism, but have worked to change it or to inform people what Jewishness really means – for my own people, for the country my parents adopted as their own, for people whose lives are unfair, impoverished, or ignored.

I first chose business, and worked very hard indeed to succeed – which I am happy to say I did – using energy and open-mindedness to get on. Many of my relatives lived in the States and I therefore did not dismiss American culture as vulgar and fly-by-night, with nothing to teach us; rather, I learnt a lot from their approach to helping each other out.

I started a business in the newly invented substance, plastic sheeting. I worked hard, and lived by a code which was based on honesty and loyalty, and which has stood me in good stead.

I made the most of commercial air travel, from its earliest beginnings. I went to India, South America, Hong Kong, all over Europe, America, Israel and Australia in planes with propellers, and loved every moment of it. I enjoyed being in the vanguard of something that made the world a smaller place.

I then chose politics, and worked feverishly to try to make it choose me. It did, in the end, although it wasn't all plain sailing. I had centuries of tradition lined up against me, most of which I relished, and some of which was holding us all back. But I like to think I brought the Conservative Party further into the twentieth century, made a great many friends inside and outside the Party, and throughout the 1970s to the present day have loved being at the heart of matters and have been able to make a contribution over forty years.

During this time, the achievements I am most proud of are Better Made in Britain, the introduction of Sunday Trading, the London Arts Season and the Festival of Arts and Culture.

I am honoured to have been made first a Knight and then a Peer of the realm, and am still working in the Lords, attending whenever there is an important vote, and also outside it, as part of a team trying to make the rebuilding of a major London hospital happen as efficiently as possible.

My family has supported me in whatever I have taken on and for that I am extremely grateful. Family is very important to me; my wife Gita and I have had a long and happy marriage, based on love for each other and our children, and a mutual tolerance aided – we both agree – by my fairly frequent absences! We celebrated our sixtieth wedding anniversary in October 2012 at the Savoy Hotel.

Our three children and their children remain the greatest pleasures of my life. We see them almost every weekend and my sons and I still go to watch Arsenal whenever they play at home!

NB I have not kept a diary over the years and therefore I hope will be forgiven if I have made any unintentional errors or omissions in writing this memoir.

CHAPTER ONE

MY EARLY LIFE

I was born in London in 1923, in a small flat over my father Philip's clothing shop in the City.

My grandfather, Abraham Feldman, was born in Wilna, Russia (now Vilnius, in Lithuania), to Morris and Rebecca Feldman. According to a beautifully written sheet of paper from Her Majesty's Principal Secretary of State for the Home Department, Abraham was born on 1 June 1874, and this valuable document was written and signed with a flourish on 7 February 1901, when he was twenty-six. He seems to have taken the Oath of Allegiance on 11 June 1901 and his certificate of naturalisation did not come cheap – costing him £5. To confirm his 'respectability and loyalty' he had four sponsors: Isaac Marks, a tailor; Edwin Falconer, a master carman; Emanuel Nathan, a butcher; and Isaac Richards, a jeweller.

My father Philip was born in 1896 and fought for his country in the First World War; family history says that he was a sniper. Handsome, with a strong character, he had something of the American about him, and, like all immigrants, he worked hard.

Starting with determination and very little else, he made a success of his commercial life, working for several years to build up his business. He set up an underwear factory in Edgware, a clothing and fabric shop and also owned cinemas in the Silvertown and Lea Bridge areas of east London. He became a Freemason, and eventually rose to be the head of his Lodge.

My father in his army uniform

My mother was from Romania, and their relationship was something of a surprise, as my father did not think much of her countrymen; he would say: 'If you shake hands with a Romanian, count your fingers!'

They were very happy and had a good marriage, and I had a happy childhood. Whereas my father was the strong one, my mother was the nurturer. She was a wonderful mother, who saw her job as looking after and protecting her children, ensuring no problems should come to us. She was also an exceptional cook, whose life's work was to have a loving family around her, all fed as much as she could get them to eat.

With my mother, in our garden

I was not always willing to oblige her, however, and she was often frustrated to find the revolting remains of my unwanted food on the pelmets and behind the piano in the dining room, where I had thrown it out of the way with no thought to the eventual results.

With Aunt Laura and cousin Billie

My sweet tooth drove my mother to distraction. She told me that she wanted to put me in a barrel of sweets and make me eat the lot to cure me of my passion for sugar. However, I fear that if she had, I would have happily worked my way through the contents; as it was, I often raided her precious wartime stock – stored on the top shelf of the cupboard – and to my family's despair, my sweet tooth remains with me to this day.

As the only boy on both sides of the family for many years, I grew up in an atmosphere of love and warmth. Yet, despite the loving and constant attention I received – especially from the women of my family – I was not above trying to attract some more.

One day, I felt like a bit more fussing, and so decided to climb down the drainpipe from a first-floor window, and pretend I had fallen. I lay there moaning most dramatically and, I thought, convincingly, and was most put out when no anxious head looked out of the window in answer to my anguished cries. I turned up the volume and eventually I was noticed and brought back in. The concern was short-lived, however, and once it was clear I was shamming, I got a whacking from my father!

I was not a pushy child, but gentle and rather shy – which surprises those who know me today. My wife insists I must have had some kind of epiphany to change me into a rather more go-getting and ambitious person; no doubt all will become clear as this book progresses.

At home, the language was English but, like all Jewish boys, I learnt to read Hebrew. My classes were long and often dreary and I decided quite early on that I could find much better things to do with the two hours I was required to spend there, and also with the money my father gave me to pay for the lessons. Instead, I decided

I would spend this money, each week, on Liquorice Allsorts and the like – that is, until the teacher contacted my parents to ask why I wasn't attending. After some severe words from my parents I started going again, but the teacher had cause to regret my attendance almost more than I did.

On another occasion, bored again, I encouraged my classmates to join me in locking the teacher out after the ten minutes' break between sessions, and there was a frightful rumpus about that. When the door was eventually opened, we were lined up to receive a caning each and, never very keen on corporal punishment, I kept sneaking to the back of the queue, hoping to avoid chastisement. I didn't. I had obviously not thought much of the teacher's intelligence, but it was quite enough to spot me scuttling to the end of the line!

All my Hebrew lessons were to prepare me for my Bar Mitzvah, which is how every Jewish boy celebrates his thirteenth birthday. Mine took place on 4 October 1936 – significant not only for the ceremony, followed by a party in a local restaurant, but also, less pleasantly, for one of Oswald Mosley's Fascist rallies, later famously known as the Battle of Cable Street.

This was an enormous rally, with Mosley's Blackshirts supported by tough yobbos ready for battle, and they were resisted violently (and ultimately successfully) by communists, Jews and pretty much everyone else in the East End.

Streets were blocked by some 10,000 police on foot and on horseback, working hard to control an estimated 300,000 people. I don't remember very clearly how we made it to the restaurant (probably in a taxi), but we managed it without injury, unlike many that day – eighty were taken to hospital and many more were given first aid where they fell. There was real fighting, and I do remember feeling pretty scared. Women threw rubbish, rotten vegetables and the contents of chamber pots at the police, and others fought with improvised weapons such as sticks, stones and chair legs.

It was significant, though, in the face of this determined resistance, that Mosley agreed to abandon the march. Routed by the East Enders, the Blackshirts thought twice about coming back.

Arsenal

I supported Arsenal, as did all my family, and each week my uncle and I would take the tube to the only station named specifically after a football team. Team Manager Herbert Chapman had the name of the tube station changed from Gillespie Road. I can remember standing with my uncle Harvey on the North Bank, with members of the crowd letting me stand in front of them so I could see. (I must have been about twelve years old at the time.)

The 1930s was a wonderful period in which to support the team, and I made the most of it. Herbert Chapman, one of the greatest managers of all time, had been appointed in 1925. By now he was at his peak, and it was Arsenal's first period of major success. Chapman made a team of averagely competent players into a dazzlingly successful one that kept on winning: the FA cup in 1930, two League Championships (in 1930–31 and 1932–33).

Chapman died of pneumonia in 1934. His replacements – Joe Shaw and George Allison – continued his good work, however, and Arsenal won three more titles (1933–34, 1934–35, and 1937–38) and the 1936 FA Cup. I was always right behind them.

School

In 1936 I won a scholarship to the Grocers' School – a venerable establishment which had been opened by the Worshipful Company of Grocers in 1876. I was very nervous at my interview with the Headmaster, Mr Balk, but I was obviously OK because soon I was in, and enjoying English and History in particular. I played football and cricket quite well and with enthusiasm.

As a boys' grammar school, Grocer's had a very good reputation. It produced several notable alumni, including Harold Pinter, Steven Berkoff (who coincidentally has written a successful play, *East*, about the Cable Street riots), and four current members of the House of Lords: myself, Baron Peston (father of BBC journalist Robert Peston), Lord Levy and Lord Clinton-Davis. Actor Michael Caine (then Maurice Micklewhite) attended for a year in 1944–45 before he was evacuated. My closest school friend was John Harris, who eventually emigrated to Israel and became a pilot in the Israeli Air Force.

Evacuation

John Harris and I were evacuated to King's Lynn in 1939 to stay with a Mrs Hanwell at 82 Wootton Road. We stayed there for a year and a half and I wrote home as often as I could. A letter I still have, sent before Christmas, explains that I will be coming home for the Christmas holidays. I imagine it is much like others I wrote. There is approving mention of a food parcel containing 'scrumptious' biscuits, and I am very concerned with the limits of a butter ration of a quarter pound, which I stress will be very much too little, if Fenella is home too. I want to buy a new bike with a dynamo for £3, 'a snip', and I am looking dutifully for batteries for my mother's torch for threepence, but these are proving 'unobtainable'.

After I returned to London, I passed an exam and attended South East London Technical College in Lewisham – emerging in 1944 as a graduate member of the Institute of Mechanical Engineering.

I invited some of my closer friends from the college, some of whom are in the photograph below, to events I organised at Edgware. One of them – Peter Prowting – turned up every few weeks, regular as clockwork.

Fellow students at SE London Technology College

CHAPTER TWO

MOWBRAY

While at college I had obviously applied myself enough to achieve my engineering qualifications, but I could not be accused of confining myself to my studies.

In my spare time I ran 'Mowbray', the Edgware Jewish Literary and Social Society attached to the synagogue, joined the local cricket club in Edgware (despite not being the greatest cricketer) and was also a member of the Lea Bridge Road choir (despite very definitely not being the greatest singer!).

Mowbray events guide

Mowbray meetings took place in the Rose Harris Hall, Mowbray, Edgware, just around the corner from home, and I have several souvenirs of its many activities, mostly from 1943.

There was a Public Meeting on 'The Fight Against Anti-Semitism'; members paid 6d and visitors 1/- to attend 'Not just another meeting, but one of great importance to Jew and Gentile alike'. Speakers included John Platts-Mills from the National Council for Civil Liberties, author and journalist Ivor Montague, and Rev W. W. Simpson, the Secretary of the Council for Christians and Jews.

Another meeting 'for the first time at any club' was Hyde Park Corner, 'when for one night, Orators Corner, Hyde Park, is transplanted to Edgware'. I had invited people whose usual podium was at Speakers' Corner, including Bible Jack ('Me and my Bible'), Dr Polypanzof ('What I Don't Know about Human Anatomy') and Jack Wright ('Millenarianism').

I still have the tickets for an All-Star Brains Trust, and for a Celebrity Dance in aid of the Home for Aged Jews, where Percival Mackey's Commodores provided the music for dancing and a specialty cabaret. This was more expensive: 4/- for members and 6/- for visitors.

The previous year my friend Elkan Allan and I had taken it into our heads to set up a major event at the Royal Albert Hall, to be called 'Meet the Giants' i.e. the five mentioned by Sir William Beveridge, founder of the National Health Service: Want, Disease, Ignorance, Squalor and Idleness – and we had inserted a sixth, Fascism. One of us would speak on this, while the other would be Chairman.

It was to be:

a mass meeting on the largest possible scale to present, ostensibly to
youth, the Giants and the means to slay them … to awaken the country
in general and young people in particular to the task which lies ahead.

The speakers I set out to attract were also giants in their fields. It
was a tall order. Elkan wrote that:

It will be seen from the proposed list of speakers that we have aimed
very high. It is only one step further to inviting Vice-President
Henry Wallace of the United States to fly over and address the
meeting from his point of view.

One of the people we invited to speak was George Bernard Shaw.
He lived in Ayot St Lawrence, and Elkan and I decided to visit
him, uninvited, travelling by Green Line bus and then walking a
further two miles to his house from where the bus had dropped us.

When we arrived, the great man was having his tea and we were
told to return when he had finished. We were allowed in after that
and were with him for about half an hour. I had taken with me his
book of *Prefaces*, which he graciously signed, but nothing I could
say would make him accept our invitation to talk.

'Oh, young people won't want to listen to me,' he insisted, and after
a while I gave up, and the audience was over. He was perfectly friendly
– after all, he could easily have slung us out – but 'No' meant 'No'.

That was the end of that idea – a pity, as I had planned a pan-
theon of the great and the good (Herbert Morrison on idleness,

with Stafford Cripps as the reserve; George Bernard Shaw on ignorance, William Beveridge on want, Edith Summerskill or Julian Huxley on disease, H. G. Wells on squalor), but after this I didn't go any further.

We also had many social events – amongst them a fancy dress party, and I can be seen, in the photograph, draping myself around the shoulders of my close friend, Maurice Ornstin.

Mowbray fancy dress party

I had also designed and printed a card which set me up for a terrific few years. Elkan, a journalist, managed to get himself invited all over the place, and I decided that I wanted a taste of all this fun too. We both had one of my impressive cards, with PRESS on them in large capital letters, purporting to come from the MET. This stood for Metropolitan European Transatlantic (which covered most bases) and for a good while we got complimentary entry into cinemas and theatres in this country and also in Europe.

PRESS

M. E. T. PRESS SERVICES

Affirm that this person,

..........B. S. FELDMAN..........,

is an authorised correspondent.
Photograph will be found on back of card.

VALID ..........................N.U.J.

(PRINCIPAL)

My Press card

I have always been passionate about film and theatre, and this encouraged Elkan and me to set up The Screen Society, a central body associating all people in Great Britain who appreciate good films. I wrote an article about the society, putting forward the reasons for its creation, namely that there was a need for films for 'a discerning few, about fifty thousand, who want more from a film than "love and kisses"'. I argue that the long queues outside the more esoteric cinemas of the time, such as the Academy and Studio One, 'seem to indicate that there is an enthusiastic public which is larger than the sources available to them'. I put forward the need to

support the interests of 'the progressive elements in the film industry' and to combat film-going apathy, suggesting that membership
be cheap and open to all, and that there should be lectures by experts
and film critics who 'would point out the highlights and faults of
the film to be shown next'. One of its main aims would be to 'encourage and sustain new talent … and [it] may also subsidise young
and promising people'.

We drew up a list of its aims and rules, and wrote for support to
such luminaries as impresario Val Gielgud (Head of Productions at
the BBC, and brother of John), and the editor of *Melody Maker*, as
well as H. A. Gottlieb, the uncle of Sheila, my girlfriend at the time.
Responses were supportive and encouraging.

Gielgud replied, asking me to submit my ideas after the war
'when there will considerably more time and space at our disposal'
– a delay but not quite a refusal.

Edgar Anstey, a Director of the Film Centre in Soho Square,
wrote to a Mr Hoellering at the Academy Cinema concerning our
discussions about the plan which he felt 'should not be dismissed
without thorough consideration'. He asked him to see me and give
me his frank opinion, and very kindly reinforced the introduction
by adding, 'We at Film Centre are anxious to help with anything of
this kind which could be put on a sound and practical basis.'

I spent some time trying to hire a venue to show films and have
meetings. I was resourceful, and not always respectful of rules and
regulations. My 1945 letter to Mr Gottlieb confesses that:

> I managed to gain access to the Royal Court Cinema, Sloane Square,
> by sneaking in through the back entrance and looked over the place

with the aid of a torch. From what I could make out in the half light, there appeared to be 400 seats in the stalls, 150 in the Dress Circle and some 300 in the Upper Circle and Gallery as well as some boxes. There is one very large room and many other smaller rooms which make the place ideal for conversion into a Film and Theatre Club. The stage is broken in one or two places and the Cinema has sustained bomb damage, which though it only appears to be superficial in the half light, may turn out to be structural, e.g. part of the front of the building is at present shored up.

Gottlieb was enthusiastic but answered that the owner, a Mr Pomeroy, would not be keen on transferring his option.

'What a pity you didn't think of this scheme of yours a little earlier. I am certain that the Royal Court Cinema is a very safe bet if it can be obtained.'

It couldn't.

Meetings were instead held in the Express Dairies Building in Edgware. The hoped-for nationwide spread of this idea never happened, but the society got off the ground and had an enthusiastic membership, albeit somewhat smaller than our big ideas.

Edgar Anstey, in *The Spectator* of 22 December 1944, records spending

a very pleasant evening with the Film Appreciation Group of a Technical Institute in south east London. Here was a group of young men/women prepared to sit down and analyse the most striking sequences of such early screen masterpieces as *Battleship Potemkin* and *The General Line*.

This did not earn us any money, but it was the birth of a passion which I later on put to very good use.

The mock by-election

An article 'Youth at the Polls', in the British and Colonial News Services, described me in the early 1940s as 'a young man with an idea', a description that has been applied to me, in various permutations, throughout my life.

I told the interviewer:

> I spend my life amongst young people … and I come across a frightening amount of ignorance and apathy. I mean to do all I can both inside and outside my club and college to dispel this. I don't care which way people think: Left or Right, up or down, it's all the same to me. What I want is to get them thinking about the things that really matter in life.

REVEILLE, FEBRUARY 14, 1944

MOCK BY-ELECTION

MICHAEL FOOT, Harry Pollitt, and Major Thorneycroft, M.P., will represent the Labour, Communist, and Conservative candidates respectively, in a mock by-election, to be run by the Edgware Jewish Literary and Social Society, on Sunday, February 20, at 7.30 p.m. Venue is the Rose Harris Hall, Mowbray-road, Edgware. Tickets, price 2s. 6d. and 5s., may be obtained from 4, Jesmon-way, Cannons Park, Middlesex.

TRIBUNE—February 18, 1944

MOWBRAY,
Edgware Jewish Youth Club,
present an imaginary
BY-ELECTION

Candidates : personal appearance of
MICHAEL FOOT (*Labour*).
HARRY POLLITT (*Communist*).
MAJOR P. THORNEYCROFT, M.P.
(*Conservative*)

on Sunday, Feb. 20th, at 7.30 p.m., at the ROSE HARRIS HALL, Mowbray Road, Edgware. (Buses 113, 141, 142, and Northern Line.)
Tickets : 5/- and 2/6 (some free seats available), at door.
Enquiries : please 'phone EDG 3162.

Advance newspaper reports on the mock by-election

I decided to organise a mock by-election at Mowbray in February 1944, and invite representatives of the main political parties to take part. It was obviously not a real by-election, but it gave the MPs a chance to air their views to an audience of some 300 people.

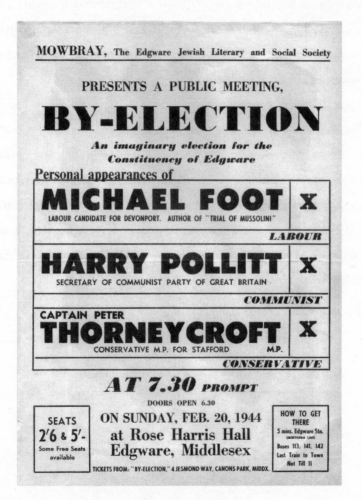

By-election poster

As always I aimed high. After all, why not? I decided to start with Clement Attlee, then Deputy Prime Minister. I looked up Mr

Attlee's number in the telephone directory (you could do that sort of thing in those days). He was a senior minister in the Government, I was a nineteen-year-old north London engineering student, running the Youth Club at the local synagogue, and the outcome was predictable, I suppose.

'How did you get my number?' he asked, and sounded rather put out when I explained. I went on to tell him my plan and asked him if he would attend.

'Certainly not,' he said firmly.

I was of course disappointed, thanked him for his time and then resolved to continue with my plans without him.

In the end, we didn't miss Mr Attlee at all as 29-year-old Michael Foot, Labour candidate for Devonport, accepted my invitation. So did Peter Thorneycroft, then the 35-year-old MP for Stafford, who agreed to represent the Conservatives, and also 56-year-old Harry Pollitt, the Secretary of the Communist Party.

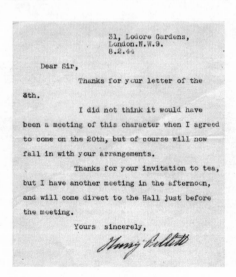

Letter from Harry Pollitt

8th February, 1944

Dear Mr. Feldman,

Thank you very much for your letter
of 4th February and for your kind
invitation.

I should be most grateful if I
could be met at Edgware Station and
will try to be there at 5.15 p.m.

Yours sincerely,

B.S. Feldman, Esq.,
96, Mowbray Road,
EDGWARE.

Letter from Peter Thorneycroft

Michael Foot, making a point

Harry Pollitt, taking questions from the audience

Thorneycroft, giving his address

I plastered the area with posters and managed to attract an audience of some 300 people, who participated energetically, putting most of their crosses in Mr Pollitt's box, much to my father's fury!

Voting

MOWBRAY THE EDGWARE JEWISH LITERARY AND SOCIAL SOCIETY

	BY-ELECTION		
	MICHAEL FOOT Labour Candidate for Devonport. Author of "The Trial of Mussolini."	*100*	
		LABOUR	
	HARRY POLLITT Secretary of the Communist Party of Great Britain.	*109*	
		COMMUNIST	
	Major **THORNEYCROFT,** Conservative M.P. for Stafford. M.P.	*53*	
		CONSERVATIVE	

Party Membership, if any

Age, if under 21

Signed

All information will be treated as strictly confidential.

Vote results

MOWBRAY'S MOCK BY-ELECTION

An audience of 350, largely Jewish, took part in a mock by-election held in the Hall of the Edgware Synagogue, and organised by Mowbray, the Edgware Literary and Social Society.

The candidates were Mr. Harry Pollitt (Communist), Major G. E. P. Thorneycroft, M.P. (Conservative), and Mr Michael Foot (Labour). None of them in his election address referred in any way to the Jews, but at question time both Mr. Pollitt and Major Thorneycroft stated their attitude towards a Jewish State in Palestine.

Major Thorneycroft said he felt himself in an uneasy defensive position, and really could not find an answer He was anxious that a working arrangement should be arrived at in Palestine, but he also felt that they could not ignore the Arabs.

Mr. Pollitt, replying to a charge that the Communist Party was sabotaging efforts to establish a Jewish State in Palestine, claimed that his Party had proved itself the best defender of the Jewish people in this country. He referred to their organised public activity against Fascism. "We differ politically in our conception of Palestine as the National Home for the Jews," he went on. "We believe that Jewish problems can only be solved on the basis of Socialism.

"I have every sympathy," he said, "with the great experiment and the constructive achievement of the Jews in Palestine. We can never be accused of any sabotage of that." His Party stood for the right of the Arabian peoples to form their own independent governments. He advocated friendship between Arabs and Jews.

The "Election" results were: Pollitt 109; Foot 100; Thorneycroft 53. Mr. Basil Feldman presided, supported by Mr. Sidney Freedberg.

Newspaper report on by-election

Everyone threw themselves into the spirit of the debate. The politicians took it seriously, and people queued up to place their ballot papers in the appropriate boxes. I suppose it was an indication of their frustration with the politicans of the day that even a mock by-election was so well patronised.

It gave people a chance to express their feelings about the times they were living in, which were not comfortable. The war was still going on and many had lost their homes and their friends and family. Needless to say, it was not a happy time in England.

I like to think that if Mr Attlee heard about it, he might have felt a twinge of regret at turning down my invitation...

CHAPTER THREE

COLLECTING HANNAH

When I was still Chairman of the Youth Club at the Edgware Synagogue I continued to organise many different and unusual events in an attempt to attract a large membership. However, by the time I reached my early twenties, I decided I should try and earn some money, and in late 1947 I made arrangements, with a friend, to go out to Poland to visit various textile manufacturers. Although it was just after the Second World War, Poland was still one of the major areas for this type of manufacturing business and we hoped we would make good contacts there.

Hannah, on arrival in the UK

As a young man I was always a keen table tennis player, and a week before we were due to travel out to Poland, I went to the synagogue to play a game, and bumped into a fellow member, Bernard Woolrich. He had relatives in Poland, and got very excited when I told him of my travel plans, asking me to find and talk to his eight-year-old cousin Hannah while I was there. I have always enjoyed doing unusual and challenging things, and so I agreed to do this, if I could find the time between our business appointments.

At the time of our visit, Poland was still very much recovering from the ravages of the war. The Communist Party had been fully in force since the January elections, and cities like Warsaw still displayed the scars of the damage that was sustained during – and after – the Nazi invasion. Food rationing was also still in place.

On arrival, we checked into the Grand Hotel – at the time the best in this rather battle-scarred area. I had a very large room, but there was no plug in the bath, and the only way to keep the water in was to wedge my heel in the plughole, and to take my bath as quickly as possible before it all ran out!

Over the next couple of days we successfully finished our business commitments and I set out to find Hannah and her father. They were just two of the many who had been in a concentration camp and at the time of our visit were living in the ghetto in Lodz, at No. 1 Ulica Noarutowicza.

Once I had tracked them down, we returned to the Grand Hotel so that we could dicsuss the possibility of my bringing Hannah back to the UK with me. Conversation, however, was rather difficult: I spoke only a little Yiddish, and Hannah spoke no English at all. Poland was a country of Slavs – a race of people Hitler considered inferior and therefore dispensable – and it was the home of one of the world's largest Jewish communities – over three million members in total. 'All Polish people will disappear from the world ... it is essential that the great German people should consider it as its major task to destroy all Poles,' said Himmler, charged by Hitler to put his plan for Aryan racial supremacy into practice. Most were killed, along with three million Polish Christians. Jews fled to the USA, the United Kingdom and elsewhere, if they could. Those who were not able to escape were enclosed in ghettos, and the Nazis took over their farms and businesses in a nation that was largely agricultural. No one was allowed to leave the country and most healthy citizens were forced into slave labour.

This would probably have been Hannah's future. Her family was so desperate to get her out of Poland and on to England that if I hadn't been able to bring her back myself they had planned to put her on a train – alone, eight years old, and speaking only Yiddish – with a placard around her neck stating her destination.

At the end of our meeting, I said that I would do all I could to bring Hannah back to the UK and after leaving some money with them to help them out, I came home. In those days children didn't need their own passports, so she could travel with me as long as I said I was a relative.

We needed to get Hannah a visa, which we applied for and which came through on my third visit. I returned to Poland at the end of January 1949 and agreed with Hannah's father that we would try to get her out of Poland by flying from Warsaw to Prague, and from there back to England.

Our well-laid plans were scuppered, however, when thick fog

meant that we were unable to fly to Prague, and had to travel by train instead. Hannah's father came with us as far as the Czech border, where he was forced off the train by the Czech guards. Hannah was distraught at this and although I had left for only a moment to get some food from the dining car, when I got back to the carriage I found her trying to climb out of the window which she had forced open. The train was going very fast by now, but this wasn't putting her off. After that particular episode I realised that I was travelling with a very frightened little girl, and I needed to keep a close watch on her.

I had a good friend in Prague – originally from England – who was married to a Czech, and whose daughter, Eva, was roughly Hannah's age. He kindly offered to look after her for me for a few days, so that I could make the final vital preparations for our return to the UK. The two girls slept on camp beds in the kitchen which was comforting for Hannah and highly reassuring for me.

Hannah and I finally got back to a drizzly England on 31 January 1949. I delivered her to her aunt and uncle – Samuel and Annie Polikoff – with a great sense of achievement. They lived on Crespigny Road in Hendon, and they were happy to take her in and give her a welcoming and loving home.

Hannah settled into her new life, and soon mastered English. I was still living with my parents, and she used to be a regular visitor to our home. We all became very fond of her, including Slipper our dog. She called him Pantoufle ('slipper' in French) and spent a lot of time playing with him. Another friend of mine sent me some American records in Yiddish which helped Hannah relax and feel more at home.

Basil, Hannah and Slipper on Hampstead Heath

Hannah met and married a remarkable man called David Lewis, a successful property developer, who has also established an amazing art collection. We have kept in close touch over the years, and in 2011 Gita and I attended their fiftieth wedding anniversary party at The Savoy.

I had one of my proudest moments when David made a speech at the dinner, explaining the part I had played in bringing his wife to this country. A lot of the people at the dinner were completely unaware that I had done this, and were frankly amazed that a young man would have had the courage to do such a thing, in those uncertain and dangerous times. Looking back on it, I am rather surprised at my bravery, but I have never regretted any of it for a moment. I am extremely proud of everything I was able to do to help Hannah and bring her to England and I am delighted that she and David remain such close and dear friends.

When I first started to write my memoirs, Hannah wrote a letter to me recalling her memories of that time – which are still vivid:

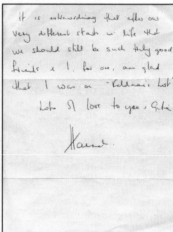

Hannah's letter to Basil

I remember you bought me a huge amount of absolutely wonderful toys in Prague, including a puppet theatre, and some wonderful boards on which you could make patterns of small pieces of shaped wood. The only thing you didn't manage to get hold of for me – and which I wanted so much – was a two-wheeled bicycle. You were absolutely wonderful to me – I remember being taken out on the donkeys on Hampstead Heath – a huge treat. I think it was that that made me decide that I was going to marry you!

You kept [in] contact with me for several years, until I began to make friends and I remember you taking me to Nursery World in Edgware High Street to buy a dress for Bernard's wedding. It was blue and white stripes, smocked in navy and I thought it was the most beautiful dress I ever had.

I came to your parents' house in Edgware quite often. They looked after me, always gave me something good to eat and I played with your dog called Slipper!

Then we met after about ten years when you were going to Poland and you wanted to know if I wanted you to look anyone up for me. I remembered you had offices off Bond Street, so I came to see you, as I was working in Park Street for the Cape Asbestos company.

I asked you to take a sweater for Lusia who helped look after me in Poland and lived with us. She was a German girl whose father was killed and whose mother left Poland for East Germany with her sister. I loved her – she was only sixteen or seventeen when she came looking for somewhere to live and she did her best for me always. I wrote to her often, but sometimes my letters were returned or came back censored. Sadly you weren't able to deliver the sweater because she was no longer at our address – in fact, she had died of cancer.

In 1967 we moved to Compton Avenue, next door to Richard Beecham, who had already left his wife Jeanette, and we became friendly with Valerie and Geoffrey Leigh. Valerie was arranging a surprise party for Richard in his new flat in Regent's Park, and asked for my help to sew up some table cloths which she was going to paint on. As we talked, I realised that Valerie knew you and Gita and when we came to the party – late as we had been to the Opera – Gita, who was in on it, came and took David off to the buffet and I sat next to you! When you saw me, you burst into tears – you realised who I was, and you simply couldn't work out what on earth I was doing there! That was quite an evening!

CHAPTER FOUR

MY FAMILY

My family, plus Sooty – our poodle – in the back garden in Hampstead

(l-r: Alex, Nick, Sooty, Gita, Basil, Steven)

My family has, and always will be, the most important thing to me. My life is so full on in many ways, and I credit all of them with keeping my feet on the ground and making so many of my successes possible.

My wife Gita is quite marvellous. She is beautiful, intelligent, a great mother, a great wife and a great help in my career. We have three children: Nicholas, Steven and Alexandra, and four grandchildren. Alex's daughter Philomena is twenty-three, Stevie's Jessica is twenty-five and Gabby is twenty-three, and Nick's Maximilian is twenty-four. They have all emerged from their respective universities with good degrees, and are out in the world of work. We see them as much as possible and they come over most weekends when they are in London.

Gita

My beautiful wife, Gita

My father was a geologist (BSc, ARCS, Imperial College London) and when we were young he worked for Shell. He had applied to join the RAF during the war, but was turned down because he had a slightly withered leg as a result of contracting polio as a child, and so his war work was to teach the RAF flying cadets navigation and maths.

I had three sisters – Coral, Janise and Helene – the 'Julius Girls'. Probably because of our father's interest in geology, I can remember us spending a great deal of time together on the coast, and also in stone quarries.

During the war we moved to the country; my mother, sisters and I spent time 'Digging for Victory'. We grew all our own fruit and vegetables and also knitted balaclavas and scarves to send off to 'the boys'. Our father was a keen sportsman who often took us to the train station – putting our bikes on the first train that arrived. We then cycled for miles back home – travelling on roads that were completely empty, apart from the occasional tank convoy and troops going off to war (all available petrol went to the army and to keep factories running).

I went to school in Berkshire, and then – when the war was over – we returned to London where I spent the last two years of my schooldays at South Hampstead High School, taking my finals before I went on to art college.

I can remember Quentin Crisp modelling for our life classes. He was an exceptional model – a delightful man and a true original. I still have many of my drawings of him from that time. Many of us students also visited Henry Moore to study sculpture, as he encouraged student help.

My art masters were largely young ex-servicemen, who later on became important in their own fields. For example, Dudley Holland started the first famous photographic department at York University and de Saumarez became a top lecturer at Leeds University.

After graduating, I taught painting and exhibited in various exhibitions such as the London Group, the Young Contemporaries etc. I was also once photographed by the press as I was carrying my paintings into the Royal Academy – fame at last!

Fenella, Rosina and friends

I knew Basil's sister – Fenella – and thought that, apart from being glamorous, she was also very amusing and determined. I also got to know Basil's cousin – Norman Howard (who later became a cancer specialist), and he invited me to one of the Oxford University balls, at which he told me about his interesting cousin, Basil – which of course piqued my interest. It was 1950 and at the time I was going out with someone else. I had read an article about Basil in one of the glossies – one of those 'young men to watch' articles, and thought 'I like the sound of him'.

Then one day my friend, Rosina, asked me to make a foursome with her boyfriend, Maurice Ornstin, and his friend, Basil. As I had nothing better to do at the time I said yes, and we went on to have a very jolly evening at Edmundo Ros's nightclub, where Basil taught me to samba. This was a new dance which Basil had been taught by an Italian girlfriend; little did I know that years later – on our honeymoon – we would be dancing it again in Brazil.

I liked Basil at once; he was handsome and smart in his beautifully tailored clothes. I remember he drove a Riley sports car,

wearing big driving gloves and a belted mac – really quite the thing!
My father, however, said that he was not the type of man who would
stay with me, as he was far too good looking.

While all this was going on in the background, I was thinking that
Gita was a very pretty girl. I had been engaged to June Gilbey, but
this had come to an end, very amicably, when she went to America,
although we kept in contact.

Gita and I went out together for a couple of years, until I decided to propose and she accepted. I asked her on Common Wood
Common, making it as romantic as my brain would allow – although I didn't go down on one knee! Her parents had obviously
been anticipating this, because when we rang home at the weekend
her father simply said, 'Well, about time!'

He interviewed me eventually, with straightforward questions
about my prospects and my plans. I was rather irritated at having to
go through all that, frankly, but it was soon over, and I passed.

The early days of our marriage

I therefore have reason to be grateful to Rosina, who was a good friend of Fenella, and who by then was PA to Laurence Olivier and Kenneth Tynan when they were starting the National Theatre.

I made up a little rhyme about her:

Rosina's demeanour
Suggests Argentina
But no, Golders Greener…

Gita recalls:

Through Basil I have met so many interesting and talented people. When he assisted Margaret Thatcher with celebrity receptions which honoured those who had made a contribution to our country, he always asked me who I would like to meet – and as a result I got to choose, and meet, my favourite authors, musicians and stars.

Basil was a great party person in those days. We gave a garden party at our home each year and he would invite soothsayers, fortune tellers, phrenologists and astrologers (including one very talented young man called Russell Grant!). Later on we would discover that many of the predictions these professionals made at our parties came true – somewhat to our surprise. We always had the most wonderful evenings, and I can't recall us ever having bad weather.

Basil's quick wit makes him a delight to be with, and once you love Basil you always love Basil. Many of his previous girlfriends stayed in touch because of his amusing ways and also his incredible loyalty. He's not a good listener, however, as his head is always so full of new ideas, and he only really takes notice if someone – or something – really interests him. When we first started going out together, I can remember telling him stories that made other people laugh, but often I could see his attention waning. However, when he wants to know about something in particular he can focus on it completely and obsessively.

Basil and Gita, at home in Hampstead

I had to be the disciplinarian in our family. The children often teamed up against me (not against each other) and they still remain close to this day. Basil's discipline, on the other hand, was pretty non-existent. I believe he saw his role was to play with them and love them. He would bounce along, filling them with enthusiasm, and they loved being with him.

He has taught me not to take everything so seriously and has certainly improved my sense of humour and tolerance. He is a very tolerant man who sees the good in people, and on the whole is an excellent judge of character.

Basil isn't, however, interested in making money for its own sake. It's the creativity, the action and the ideas that excite him. He is also not a gambler - unlike the 'big boys' who always have to be one step ahead of each other. Nor is he ruthless – he's honourable and decent and incredibly loyal, which hasn't always worked in his favour. He doesn't discard people.

Basil reduced his business activities when he decided to enter politics – and I have to say that this came as a surprise to me as I had no idea that he intended to do so!

I should have expected that he would do something like this because he has always been into making a difference to the community, even as a boy. That's why he has included a phoenix in his coat of arms to symbolise the fact that he is reborn every day. He has always been unbelievably energetic – and even now, aged ninety-one, he is still working many days at the office, and also in the Lords where he takes part in debates on Lords Reform etc.

Basil is not, however, really a team player – he likes to be in charge so that he knows that things will actually get done.

After we had our three children I did charitable work in hospitals and with old people, and later trained to become a Marriage Guidance Counsellor with LMGC – the London Marriage Guidance Council (which Basil encouraged me to do).

I worked in health centres all over London and in Harley Street and it was very educational and also fascinating work. We constantly improved the way our movement worked as we learnt more, and eventually we started to branch out into doctors' surgeries. In time, LMGC were very influential in starting up Relate.

Gita's recipe for a long and happy marriage?

> Both our expectations were the same (although never discussed) and we have always put our family first. Also, because Basil often had to travel abroad quite a lot, we both had a lot of space in which to do our own thing.

My children

My three children are – after the usual vicissitudes of adolescence and young adulthood – all close. We see each other regularly, and enjoy each other's company. I still go to watch Arsenal with my two sons, as I have done for at least fifty years. When my father was still alive, he came too.

Nick

Nick is the eldest. He has been extremely successful in the music business, being one of the two core members of the band Wang Chung.

Nick, aged five

He was a star at his prep school – St Anthony's – and then went on to Hereward House, where he was Head of School and Sports Captain. From age thirteen until A Levels, he was at Highgate School, and from there went to Liverpool University to read Psychology, although this wasn't a great success. He lasted a couple of years, before coming back to London and a pretty worrying existence including a complicated girlfriend, living in a King's Cross squat, and a series of undemanding jobs. This was until he realised that he could make music, and make it pay.

Gita and I weren't too happy about his idea of going into the music business, although we ended up being proved wrong – as he has made a great success of it.

As Nick recalls:

I crashed and burned at university, and when I came back my parents must have been really worried about me. They would sit me down every so often and have a chat making really strong and intelligent points with which it was very hard to disagree, so I would sit there feeling inadequate.

One day they turned up in the Rolls to see if they could rescue me from my squalor. The older I got, the more my sense of not achieving increased. I withdrew.

They could be quite formidable. Dad would make me feel I was a bit of an idiot; not unkindly, and I totally get it now – but then, although I knew it made a lot of sense, it made me feel pretty inadequate. I can see it in my son, Max, who is twenty-one and at university doing English and History – I have tried to let go while giving him encouragement and hoping everything will be all right.

I didn't want to go into business like Dad, but wanted to do my own thing. I always felt he was loving and caring, and he never smacked me, except once when he had obviously been told to – it was a pretty half-hearted attempt!

When I was about fourteen, I remember very clearly going for a walk with him. I had some extreme view – probably about hypocrisy. He calmly pointed out that everything is a question of degree. You don't have to be either this or that; there is stuff in the middle. This hadn't really occurred to me.

Dad showed me interesting ways of looking at things. We didn't talk all the time, but there has always been something good there between us.

Nick found a job booking bands for DJM Live Music Agency, and then he had a go doing it off his own bat, and things began to happen. He discovered and signed Adam and the Ants in the early '80s, all pirate clothes and white lace, and stripes on the face.

He was very much part of the New Wave in the 1980s, and his band Huang Chung was successful, mostly in North America; they were signed by Arista Records to make two albums in early 1981. Nick had adopted, for some reason best known to himself, the name Nick de Spig. They all had pseudonyms – Jeremy Ryder was Jack Hues, and Darren Costin was Darren Darwin (later just Darwin).

After the first album of the two-album deal they moved to Geffen Records, and became only the second UK-based act to be signed to them worldwide. It was Geffen who suggested they change their name from Huang to Wang Chung. It was around this time they dropped the pseudonyms too.

Nick recalls:

I got a job as a booker/agent. I lied my way into it really. I did it
for two years, but didn't really hack it. I started to get Adam and
the Ants shows, and I rather half-heartedly got into punk with my
shorter bouffant hair style – I probably looked terrible, bouffing
about the place. Then I moved out of the relationship and the flat,
and left the job – I knew I was better than many of the people I
was booking out. I decided to do it myself and take the risk. And
it was a risk. I had no money coming, no deal, and so I put an ad in
Melody Maker.

This started my long and insecure path to having any success,
which lasted about four years, during which time I worried a lot, and
thought perhaps I had been deluding myself. It had only been a few
years really since I had been head of everything at school, and now it
was a very different story. My parents' expectations had fallen.

But things started happening eventually. They drew a long breath
of quiet relief and never said 'We told you so!'

I remember attending a dinner for Designers at Debenhams at the
British Fashion Council Awards in 1984, the same night Nick was
on *Top of the Pops* with his band Wang Chung, and their hit, 'Dance
Hall Days'. I introduced myself to my neighbour, who was wearing
a pretty dress and rather a lot of make-up:

'Basil Feldman,' I said, holding out my hand.

It was grasped firmly. 'Steve Strange,' came a deep voice. 'I'm
a musician.'

'So is my son,' I told him proudly, when the feeling had come back into my hand.

The band has also written the music for films, including *To Live and Die in LA*, which became their third album, going into the American Top Ten on the soundtrack chart.

Nick has also worked on the other side of the music business: as A&R manager for Warner Music UK, working with Suggs of Madness, with whom he wrote the lead track for the movie *Hollywood Avengers*, and the band Black Star Liner, Mercury Music Prize nominees in 1999.

Now he continues to play in places like Japan and Las Vegas, to considerable crowds of people who are, it seems, prepared to pay for the privilege of hearing him and Jack Hues play and sing. Most recently Wang Chung appeared at the 2012 UK Rewind Festivals in Scone Castle and Henley-on-Thames.

Nick comments:

Dad is a great networker. He is really good at setting things up and does it even now. He just talks to people, whoever they are, and can instantly connect. It was because of him I went to Downing Street for the first time, and found myself listening to the lead singer of Yes, John Anderson, who explained in great detail his theories about fairies and their existence. If I had wanted to invent a successful, slightly off-the-wall rock star, he would have been it!

Things have worked out very well, although nobody can rest on their laurels. At the peak of my success, sitting in New York, with 'Everybody Have Fun Tonight' at number two in the US charts, talking to a big producer, everything felt overwhelmingly ridiculous and unreal. I remember thinking, 'I am just an imposter. This is little me.'

Everyone should feel this way – it makes people human and reminds them that being a big, important guy is not all there is to life. And nor is it a given. It took me a long time to get anywhere, and it hasn't all been plain sailing for Dad either. It says a lot for his strength of character and humanity that he is where he is, the subject of so much affection from his family and his many friends and colleagues.

Gita and I get together regularly with both Nick and with his son Max who is now twenty-four and enjoying his career as a budding journalist.

Alexandra

Alex with her very proud Daddy, aged three

My daughter Alex is beautiful and talented – as is her daughter, Philomena, who has just graduated from Sussex University with a first class degree in English.

Alex trained as a graphic designer. She has always been passionate about art, and as a child she and Gita spent a lot of time together drawing and painting.

Alex recalls:

> My mother read us Dickens and took us to art galleries and played us Mozart – so we were exposed to all sorts of culture from an early age. She was a painter too, so what artistic ability I have I expect I got from her.

Alex did her first degree at St Martin's College of Art. This was hardly a surprise, although we didn't really want her to go to art college, if truth were told. However, she has made us eat our reservations.

As Alex remembers:

> I enjoyed St Martin's and worked hard there. My parents would send the Rolls round to collect me and my portfolio at the end of each term, and I would be overcome with embarrassment and tell the driver to wait around the corner!

Next she did a postgraduate degree at the London College of Printing and qualified with a distinction in Advanced Typography. It looked lovely, but frankly Gita and I couldn't really see the point of all the effort she put into producing beautiful lettering which could have been done by machine in a fraction of the time.

Alex:

I had my postgraduate degree show in Elephant and Castle, to which my parents came of course. I showed my father all my careful lettering, which I had sweated blood over. I told him it had been done by hand, expecting him to understand how long it had taken and what an achievement I felt it was.

'How bloody stupid!' he said.

For him, it was a waste of time, and could have been done much more quickly on a computer!

When I had qualified, I worked for various design consultancies. Then Dad suggested I contact someone at a big finance house called Guidehouse and they gave me the job of designing their whole identity. Inspired by this, I started my own consultancy, got another big client and off I went. I also did design work for English Heritage.

Dad was always happy to write introductory letters for me, and was full of ideas and contacts to approach. It's the way he is. He has no problem asking, and so helped me a great deal. I went all over the place to pitch to people. Often, though, all they wanted to do was to talk about him!

I went to see a really important man in Northern Ireland, whom everybody was scared of, and was invited to have lunch with him. I was very excited at the prospect, but in fact all he did was ask about Dad.

I met my husband, also a designer, and we ran our own successful business together. Then, when I had Philomena, I decided to take a back seat for a while, and now I work as an ad hoc project manager and consultant.

I was very busy when Alex was growing up, but not too busy to vet all her boyfriends and give her my unvarnished opinion of them. I am not sure she took any notice, but I did not hesitate to tell her what I thought.

My parents were very forthright in their opinions. Dad certainly didn't hesitate to tell me that So and So was not right for me – not that I took very much notice at the time.

I remember one day I wanted to introduce a new boyfriend whom I thought was wonderful. I was all dressed up to go out, waiting for him to arrive. I let him in, and Daddy was coming down the stairs. I said, 'Daddy, this is…' but he just walked straight past and ignored me. Not because he was being horrid, he just had something else on his mind.

My mother paces herself with my father who is always preoccupied with another new idea or project. They both have lists – hers are on small pieces of paper, and his are distinctive – on yellow paper, and he keeps lots of copies.

Daddy is a very special person. We were always close but never spoiled, although of course we didn't go without. He roped us into all sorts of things – when he went into politics we had our photograph taken as a family and I was terrified that someone would see me – I was at that age when being cool mattered more than anything. But we all did it, for him!

I left the discipline to Gita, as she will be the first to tell you. She was very involved with the children and did all sorts of interesting things with them. I enjoyed them all enormously. I was running a successful business when they were small, but made as much time for them as I could.

Daddy was brilliant when we were little, and he was brilliant with my daughter. He would get his driver to drop him off at my flat around 6.30 in the evening so he could spend time running up and down and playing with Philomena and do all the physical cuddly stuff he had done with us when we were small. When she went to school, Philomena came back one day and told me that they had thanked Grandpa at the end of assembly. 'Thanked Grandpa? Whatever for?' I asked her.

'I don't know, but we said a prayer and thanked the Lord.'

I am now a volunteer Blue Badge guide at the Tate, which is fantastic. As a member, I was invited to consider volunteering, and told it would be an informal interview. I therefore walked insouciantly into a room to face a terrifying row of people to whom I had to make a presentation about a painting – I chose Millais's *Ophelia*. After I had finished, they asked me a whole lot of questions, including what I thought was the most important personal quality. 'Charm,' I said – inspired by both my parents, who have it in bucket loads.

I now guide at Tate Modern and Tate Britain taking people on my own themed tours of the collection. I spent 2013 training as a guide to the City of London, learning about every aspect of the City, and have just launched my own business taking people on bespoke

London art tours. In February 2014 I was also delighted to be given the Freedom of the City of London.

Steven

Steven, learning to ride his cycle aged three

When my younger son Steven came out of Manchester University, where he had studied Management Sciences, I hoped he might enjoy business as much as I did.

I had bought a company – Solport – a few years earlier which looked as if it might do well, if it had someone sensible to run it and bring it into the twentieth century. I hoped that this might be Steven; it was a good place for him to start and once he had settled in and learnt about it, and I hoped he might consider running it one day.

He was happy enough to consider the proposition, until I told him where it was – Goring on Sea, or 'Boring Goring', as he would learn to call it. But that was that – nothing I could do about its location.

He decided to have a go, and moved down to Brighton to be nearby. He had already done some work for me, so I was happy to ask him to help me with this company.

The company had been going for 120 years, and had the back catalogues to prove it, with drawings of all the stuff it sold. These were styptic pencils, eye patches, finger stalls: all the things that people need but don't talk about much. They had traded with the Boots company for years and their orders used to arrive with the cheques attached. Solport supplied their products all over the world, in various outposts of the Empire, and our agents were Major General So-and-So in Nigeria or in the Sudan.

It was an import/export manufacturing business with a factory at the back of the offices. I put Steve straight on to the manufacturing floor and he went through the whole business process.

In those years I discovered a different side to my father. I was interested in expanding my business knowledge and he was interested in helping me do just that. He would come down once a month or so, just turning up in the way he does, and he was – as always – absolutely brilliant at it all. We laughed all the time; I hadn't realised how funny my dad was – in business too. It was a revelation. He used to say things to the management with a straight face, and I often had to hide a smile. They didn't always get his humour, but it really made me laugh.

But it wasn't all a giggle; he took it seriously too, and would become not just my dad, but this man who was creative, excellent at design, able to spot an accounting mistake at twenty paces, someone who understood the market and how to get the best out of the people who worked for him.

I made Steve a significant shareholder and then suggested he travel the world.

In the second year, Dad suggested I go to the Far East on my own and check out the market there, meet the people we were doing business with, and tell him all about it. I did, and found out that buying and selling is in my blood. My dad has always believed in me, and he has taught me that it doesn't matter what you do. What matters is that you apply your mind, get on with it, work hard, and if it's meant to happen it will.

I was away for six weeks, and pulled off some big sales and some big deals. It was absolutely mind-blowing and I had a great time. I went to Singapore, Malaysia, Taiwan, Korea, and found myself selling to Company A and buying from Company B in the morning, and in the afternoon doing it the other way around.

I worked hard to make money for the business, and this wasn't easy as there was a terrible recession at the time, wages were expensive and people were going direct to the manufacturers in the Far East. We made money from products we manufactured, and I found a range of American support products (let's not go there) which had been poorly distributed by Gillette in the UK and hadn't been selling. The product was absolutely fine, it just hadn't been pushed so we took it over, reboxed it, and sent it out again – and it sold so much so that the American manufacturer wanted to buy the company and use it as their European base and manufacturing centre.

That's when I really saw my dad move into action. I don't know how he did it, but he charmed the company into buying our business, and at a price that was so way beyond what I expected that it was quite astounding!

There was a bit of to-ing and fro-ing, which always happens in big company takeovers, and we were eventually bought by the Jung Corporation. I spent some time in the business for the next year, helping some of their export markets. They wanted to lay off our business, and soon afterwards came the end of my time in Boring Goring.

I now work for myself, largely in the care home and hospital property market. I have learnt so much from my father, and he has been so much better at business than I could ever be. If I had a problem and approached him with it, he listened, put an idea through his head, and then offered advice in a very non-judgemental way. He is very clever, unbelievably diplomatic; a full-on entrepreneur to his finger tips. But it isn't about the money – it's all about creativity. Of course money is nice to have but he is more interested in using his head, and in the strategy and in winning.

He's a big thinker.

He updated the Tory Party which used to be run, very much, by the 'blue rinse brigade' (perhaps not the men), he understood young people, and was aware of the power of celebrity. Nobody had done celebrity politics before. No one had had T-shirts saying 'Vote Basil Feldman' on the front and 'I care' on the back.

All his ideas are innovative in this way, and it's always a pleasure doing business with and for him. I love him to bits; he has been my hero all my life.

Steven has two wonderful daughters – Jessica and Gabriella. When she was small, Jessica wrote a heart-warming and highly flattering essay at school about me:

He was knighted by the queen then he became a lord he became a lord because he helped the world he gave money to the poor and he does not get cross. He is also a hero because he made me in a way he made my daddy and without my daddy I wouldn't be alive and he cares about everything he can't bear to throw anything away so he gives it to me he does not just care about people he also cares about toys and things like that ... I love him he is part of my family and he helps me in lots of ways like looks after me when my mum and dad go out pays money to buy me things takes me down to Hampstead and no other Grandpa is like mine and no other Grandpa byes you everything you want [*sic*].

Not true in every detail, especially regarding my financial generosity, but I obviously did something right!

Fenella

Basil and Fenella

My sister Fenella was born several years after me. We were close as children, and there are photographs of us by the sea, including a rather alarming one of the two of us sitting on the back of a stuffed tiger in Cliftonville, Kent. We had a nanny then, very severe in her starched uniform; I remember she took me down to the sea in my pyjamas one day, which did not go down very well with my parents.

Basil and Fenella on the beach at Cliftonville

Fenella went on to do very well at North London Collegiate School and was much admired within the family. Then she dropped a bombshell that changed everything. She declared that she was going to be an actress – a professional actress, on the stage and in front of a paying audience if she had anything to do with it! She might as well have said she wanted to become an astronaut, or a poisoner…

She says that the family wanted her to be a nice girl with lots of children, married to a nice man. This is not at all what she had in mind, preferring to paint her face and go on the stage and say things, as she told BBC's Jenni Murray.

The family – all of them – went berserk. She remembers a posse of large black cars driven by various Feldman relatives who turned up to try to dissuade her most forcefully. There was little doubt in their minds that they could do this, but they hadn't reckoned on Fenella's force of character. She is not tall, and she is both beautiful and glamorous, and always has been, so she may have looked like a pliable young woman who would do what she was told. They soon realised their mistake.

'Fine,' she said, and applied to drama school.

She won a scholarship, and worked hard there for a year. She fed and clothed herself by living extremely frugally, and she tells me that if I played any role at all I kept the family off her back. Not enough, however.

In an interview for *The Independent* in 2008, she told Robert Chalmers:

I had to hide every morning, until Daddy had gone out to work. And then stay out late to try to avoid him in the evening – because of these terrible rows. Mummy would come and try to get me to go back home in the middle of the day. After about a year the school said, look, this cannot carry on. I had to leave.

As a young girl, she had wanted to be a doctor, she told Chalmers.

I remember once saying that I'd like to go to university. My father told me: 'I would rather see you dead at my feet than have you go to a university.' I'm laughing about it now, but at the time I was terribly upset. I didn't even understand what going to university meant.

However, medicine's loss was theatre's gain. She was given her first part by Ron Moody and it wasn't long before she was appearing with Kenneth Williams who, she says, gave her a very tricky time. 'I used to be innocent, I used to be trusting, but after eighteen months of that...'

Apparently he was a delight when he allowed himself to be, but if he wasn't feeling like it, it was not easy sharing a stage with him.

It was lovely when he would let you in. I would say that, in that medium, I wouldn't have wished to work with anybody else. We would egg each other on and on and on. It was divine. But if he didn't feel like it, he would revert to original script and it would be 'oh it's another of those nights'.

Fenella being Fenella, and a Feldman, kept at it. Her career blossomed and she became a household name. In 1959 she was extremely good in *Valmouth*, by Sandy Wilson. She is generally known as the queen of the double entendre (her voice says it, even if the words do not), a reputation which, although delicious, would not have pleased our parents.

Fellini was very keen on her although (in what she acknowledges was her biggest mistake) she turned down the chance to work with him in a film because she had accepted a role at Chichester. Fellini wanted her to play the incarnation of six different men's desires. She appeared on several Morecambe and Wise shows in the 1970s and also in their 1972 Christmas Show – all the while working hard not to collapse with laughter.

As Fenella recalls:

> It was wonderful working with Morecambe and Wise, because they wanted you to be good. They were marvellous and knew exactly what was what. Every now and then Eric would get sick of a very good line, and replace with it another good line and before we knew it, the whole script had been rewritten.
>
> I made up my mind I would keep a straight face. I didn't want to upset them by looking as if they couldn't make me laugh so I worked out a thing where I would pretend I had slightly corpsed. And it worked.

One of her most memorable roles, of course, was as the sultry Valeria in *Carry on Screaming* where, after asking a startled Harry H. Corbett if he minded if she smoked, she spontaneously combusts, disappearing in a thick grey cloud.

She has always had charisma, and her darkly cosseting voice, with a hint of a laugh in it, remains instantly recognisable. Patrick

McGoohan asked her to be the announcer in *The Prisoner* but not to be too sexy... She accepted for seven episodes, always uncredited.

Listening to her on *Just a Minute* talking about soirées is one of the highlights of radio in my opinion! Nicholas Parsons is beside himself with laughter, and so is Kenneth Williams.

Jenni Murray interviewed Fenella in February 2011, just before the opening of her latest play, *Dearest Nancy, Darling Evelyn* which is based on the letters between Nancy Mitford and Evelyn Waugh. She opened by saying that Fenella's voice is the only one that she has ever envied, and asked her whether it was nature or nurture – Fenella says the former and I agree. She sounded like a star long before she ever became one. The play – and Fenella's performance – was very well received. She was described as a deliciously sharp and malicious Nancy, and she agreed that Nancy could be very cutting but did it so sweetly that many people didn't realise what she was doing.

Always unpredictable, Fenella has not confined herself to traditional acting roles. She was the supercomputer in the video game *Martian Gothic* in a script written by science fiction author Stephen Marley. Since 2000 she has been recording with Savoy, a book publishing and recording company, reading works by Colette, J. G. Ballard's *Crash* and T. S. Eliot's *Four Quartets*.

She made an album of cover songs including Robbie Williams's 'Angels', Kylie Minogue's 'Can't Get You Out of My Head', New Order's 'Blue Monday' and the White Stripes' 'Passive Manipulation'. She has also provided the voice to two tracks on writer-performer Graham Roos's album *Quest*, was Sandalphon in his verse cabaret *Apocalypse Calypso*, and most recently provided a substantial cameo in *Darkness*, his abandoned film about Byron. In 2006, she toured Ireland in *The Vagina Monologues*.

Fenella is a patron of the theatre charity The Music Hall Guild of Great Britain and America and wrote the foreword to *Carry On Actors* (*The Complete Who's Who of the Carry On Film Series*) by Andrew Ross in 2011.

We were close as children, as I have said, but then our lives took over for a while. I was setting up a business and being a politician and a family man, while she was building up her career.

She has never married although she has almost done so once or twice. In her thirties she had a passionate relationship with a man she describes as remarkable, but they never tied the knot.

Tellingly, she told an astrologer that

I reasoned that if I was established as an actress when I met someone, it would be an essential part of me – no one could take it away. But of course, it doesn't always work out like that, and you can't always arrange these things.

My cousin, Billie Harris, recently visited the UK and I got Fenella and other relatives together for lunch at the Lords to celebrate Billie's eightieth birthday. The head waiter was a Fenella fan and got so excited that his attention was distracted for most of the meal!

We both share a sort of determination, possibly because of our upbringing and parents, and certainly because we are energetic and focused, qualities that have worked for us both. We see each other regularly now, of course, and she continues to work – a considerable achievement after fifty years of stage and screen.

I am still often amazed by her; she is a real star.

My wonderful sister

CHAPTER FIVE

INTO BUSINESS

At the beginning of the 1940s, I was in my late teens and my father was quite keen for me to go out to work, so I got the local paper and started looking.

A small firm of accountants was looking for a young man to work for them, so I rang up to make an appointment. I got on my bike and rode down to Hendon to see them as agreed, and found H. W. Fisher, a very small practice in a private house. The boss, Harold Fisher, interviewed me and told me I could start whenever I liked. I would be paid 5/- a week, and expected to work five weekdays and Saturday mornings. It was a Wednesday, and I started immediately.

I had been very low key, and not asked how much I was going to earn, so on Saturday I heard my name.

'Feldman.'

'Yes sir.'

'When did you start?' although he knew perfectly well.

'Wednesday morning, sir.'

He put his hand in his pocket, and I felt pretty hopeful. I had had a good start and now he was going to show me his appreciation. He took out 3/- and fourpence, which he carefully handed over, coin by coin. He had worked it out to the last penny: I had worked for three a half days out of five and a half, so that was what he owed me from my weekly wage of five bob. You mean, miserable old devil, I thought. When I get older, I'll use your firm and give you a hard time.

I worked for him for just over a year and a half, cycling to work through bomb-damaged streets – the eerie sight of half-collapsed houses on either side serving as another reminder of the war on our doorstep.

I was occasionally sent to visit clients, which was quite surprising, as I was only a kid. I did my best to help them with tax and that sort of thing, and I remember one of the émigrés saying to another, '*Gib ihm zehn*' which meant give him 10/-. This happened a few times – a few quid here and there, which meant a lot to me. I met all sorts of people, some who were mean and some who were helpful and kind. It was a good lesson in how to treat people.

I was true to my resolve. I used H. W. Fisher as my accountants when I went into business, and I still use them today.

After Fishers I applied for a job at the Press Association which said I would be dealing with matters all over the world. I got the job, but on my first day I found 'all over the world' meant putting articles in pigeonholes marked with the names of the countries they were about. I left after two days. Another good lesson – that not everything is as it is presented.

The Screen Society Elkan and I had set up may not have taken England by storm, but it gave us more ideas still. In 1944 he and I approached the army's Regional Committees for Education with a syllabus for Engineer Cadets who were undertaking a 21-month course. The Board of Education had decided two hours out of the thirty-seven and a half each week were to be spent on non-technical subjects and we were only too happy to help them fill these.

We received a response from Harry Ross, Assistant Secretary, who called it 'admirable, both in its comprehensiveness and the way it is arranged' and obviously passed it on.

The syllabus encompassed lectures, film appreciation, public speaking, gramophone recitals (with music from Mozart to swing, and more swing), novelty items (including a quiz, poetry and prose with comments from the author, a mock trial and a balloon debate), theatre visits, discussions and play readings.

A month later, the Sgt Education send me a note offering me 10/- an hour to visit south London sites as a Lecturer-Discussion Leader: 'My Battery is very inadequately served and I should be grateful if you would undertake the work,' he wrote, and soon I was paying what I earned into my Post Office savings account with satisfaction. This was not big business but it was a start.

I made other forays into the world of commerce which had, quite honestly, not been a roaring success. I had tried to recruit some people to help me sell firewood – an enterprise which lasted all of a couple of days, rather like my entry into the world of real estate; I found selling houses considerably harder than it appeared.

From little acorns

Then business began, if not exactly to boom, but to take off gently. At Mowbray, I had met someone called Richard Beecham and we'd got on well. I heard the firm of Johnson and Philips had some 'metally' sort of stuff spare – Heaven knows what it was – but I rang them and asked if they would like to sell it.

'Normally not,' they told me, 'but OK, you can have it for £1,000.'

I told my father about the deal and asked if I could borrow the money. To my delight he agreed. We went down with a couple of lorries, picked it up, and we managed to sell it for a good profit.

Later on Richard Beecham, David Duncan (who had changed his name from David Dubno) and I went into business together doing all sorts of things – I suppose we were in our early twenties.

We spent some time thinking about where we could make a decent profit, and looked hard at the market and what was new and interesting.

Plastics were essentially invented in the war and we thought (correctly) there might be a profit in something that was still so new. I am not sure it was glamorous, but it was something that people needed, and so we decided to make the most of demand and supply. This is something I have applied throughout my life, in business and in politics, and it has always served me well.

We manufactured and distributed, and this led later to my travelling all over the world looking for places to buy and to sell – and also to see as much of the world as possible and have a really good time.

We played around with bath caps, I remember, and we got a big order from Woolworths for chemists' sundries – those things on a stand like scissors and tweezers and so on. It was an enormous order, and they asked if they could come and see our factory.

Factory? What factory?

Undaunted, we hired one for three days, and put up an important-looking sign over the door which read: 'Field Maine'. Various ladies we knew, including my sister Fenella, another female relative and Richard's wife assiduously inspected these mysterious toilet bags and the like, and the man from Woolworths said fine.

Years later, I met him again and reminded him of this.

'Did you know we had no factory?' I asked him.

'Of course I did,' he replied, 'but I just wanted to help you.'

Things went pretty well for some time. My father had guaranteed an overdraft of £1,000 to get us off the ground and I had been living at home so there were not many living expenses. I didn't get married until I was twenty-nine so London was a lot of fun and I was going out with plenty of girls. We worked very hard and built up a reasonable amount of money and a successful little business based on PVC sheeting.

By 1946 or so, I had a small, comfortable office in the City with stylish furniture that I enjoyed using. I like design, and have collected all sorts of bits and pieces over the years that have caught my eye. Some have turned out trumps: I have some of the first chairs Eames designed, for instance.

Dunbee

In 1948 we moved to larger premises in Bond Street, and Isadore Shulman was added to our small team as Finance Director. We also employed Mr Paddock, who moved bales of cloth and drove our car.

In 1952, after I married, the office moved to Great Portland Street and between us we did rather well – at least at first. By then we were Dunbee Combex Marx, which consisted of a toy company which Richard ran, and another one, Field Maine (of the sign over our fake factory door), that dealt with plastics, DIY and plant hire and was my responsibility.

I would be collected in a car to start work each day at what I considered the crack of dawn, and got to the office at what felt to me like the middle of the night. I have never been a lark – I have my best ideas in the still watches of the night, and much prefer to work later.

Dunbee had as its Chairman the delightful Scottish grandee Lord Westwood who would start every speech with the same phrase, which raised a smile every time he used it: 'As Henry VIII said to each of his wives, I won't keep you long.'

We were by this time running a business that seemed, on the face of it, extremely successful, and in many ways it was. However, it had not happened just like that – I had really put my back into it. I suppose I was one of the first DIY and plant hire people, and Richard Beecham wanted to go into toys. By the 1970s, Richard had bought many of the toy companies in the world, which seemed like a good idea at the time, but it turned out to be too ambitious, and things went a bit awry.

As it turns out, I am glad I concentrated on my side of the business: I burned my fingers rather less than Richard did and could carry on, although we all lost a great deal of money.

It was not a happy time, and as a result we went our separate ways.

CHAPTER SIX

DOUGLAS HAYWARD
SUITED ME

O ne of my more interesting sidelines happened almost by accident. I was still working with Beecham and Duncan when I saw one of Douglas Hayward's suits in a 1967 edition of *Harpers and Queen*. He had recently set up in Mayfair, and had been picked up by the magazine – and soon most of fashionable London. Liking what I saw of his style, I invited him to come and see me. I was impressed, commissioned him to make me a suit, and so a long friendship began. Later, I discovered that his wife (or girlfriend as she was then) was one of my employees!

We did very well together. I gave him business ideas, and eventually he asked me to buy half his business. This continued to be a pleasing adjunct to the rest of my turbulent business life.

Douglas Frederick Cornelius Hayward was the son of a man who cycled into the BBC before dawn to tend the boilers, and then washed buses at the Uxbridge depot, before cycling back to the family semi in Hayes, which he had painted shocking pink. He enjoyed his topiary, which was displayed in the front garden.

Douglas's accent, in his early career, stopped him getting a job in Savile Row. Instead, he worked at a tailor's in Shepherd's Bush where he made suits for up and coming actors such as Terence Stamp and Peter Sellers.

He moved on to Dimi Major in Fulham, who made Ronnie Corbett's suits, and then set up on his own in Pall Mall, taking his first order after a very silent and unsettling ten days.

He was married to Diana, the sister of Melissa Stribling who was the wife of film director Basil Dearden, and this connection was very helpful in making contacts with rising stars. He began to do well, and often would drive his old Mini up west, to the Dorchester Hotel to see customers such as Richard Burton. Even though he was becoming popular, and as a result, well off, he remained proud of his Cockney heritage and visited his mother every week, leaving her £1 for her meals on wheels. After her death in 1984, the £1 notes were found in fifteen ice cream boxes under her bed, with a note: 'This money is to get Doug out of prison when they finally get him.'

She could not believe that his income came only from tailoring, but was convinced that he had to be involved in something shady as well.

He liked to get together for an old-fashioned knees-up, complete with bread pudding competitions and fish and chips, and would sometimes take himself and friends off to Southend. He loved football and beer, and supported Fulham and Arsenal, and watched Chelsea after a good lunch on the King's Road. He set up his own team, The Mount Street Marchers and Social Club, and talked clients such as Richard Harris, Tom Courtenay and sometimes Bobby Moore into playing for it. The team played in arranged matches in Hyde Park on Sunday mornings, but he persuaded the Rank

Organisation to pay for them to fly to Mexico for the 1970 World Cup. They did so, expecting an exclusive documentary about the England team. What they got was footage of Doug and Co. in games against local park sides...

In 1967 he moved to 95 Mount Street, living above the shop, and spending weekends in Oxfordshire on Lord Hambleden's estate.

His voice (slightly modified) was an asset rather than a hindrance, adding to the unstuffy atmosphere of his shop, and he made clothes for (amongst many others) Michael Caine, Roger Moore, Jackie Stewart, John Gielgud, Rex Harrison, Lord Hanson, Mark Birley – and me. Oh and Bianca Jagger, although he was uncomfortable fitting her suits. Amazingly, he was also the model for Harry Pendel, the main character in Le Carré's *Tailor of Panama*.

His shop – with grey flannel on the walls and Italian marble floors – became a sort of salon frequented by anyone he knew who was passing. It was not unusual to meet Kirk and Michael Douglas, Michael Parkinson and the Duke of Abercorn all being fitted for suits and enjoying a chat. Joan Collins would drop in, and they decided to call themselves 'The Mayfair Orphans', which of course Doug loved.

He used to sit in a great big chair in the middle of the room, with Bertie his Jack Russell beside him, and dispense tea and tales. He never made a suit for someone he didn't like.

The photographer Terry O'Neill once said: 'They call Doug "The Buddha of Mount Street". You wouldn't believe the number of people who go to him for advice. He's probably the best-loved man in London.'

His suits were completely recognisable: I was delighted when Gita told me that I looked like James Bond until she qualified it: 'from the back'. His own were often in colourful tweed, and he also sold handmade shoes and his own line of watches and leather luggage.

He designed suits for Laurence Harvey in *The Spy with a Cold Nose*, Terence Stamp in *Modesty Blaise*, Noël Coward in *Boom!* and Michael Caine in *The Italian Job*.

Nick recalls:

I can remember Doug calling at the house to see Dad – and he always had a glamorous woman on his arm. On one occasion I remember he came with Bianca Jagger, and on another with Linda Thorson (who – at the time – was one of the Avengers).

I invested in a restaurant he opened in London, together with Patrick Lichfield, called Burke's. It was a dining club, serving a mixture of posh and boarding school food, and was decorated by Stanley Kubrick's wife, Christiane. I am not sure it ever made much money but we all had a lovely time. Lichfield took him to Mustique to entertain Princess Margaret:

Nobody ever knew what to do with Margaret. Doug was always wonderful with her. He knew the words of every song Cole Porter ever wrote. He was the only one who could sing duets with her and never miss a beat.

His secret? He told Peter Evans of the *Daily Mail* it was to treat her like 'a regular bird. You can't run with those people and worry how it's going to play out.'

Douglas's second wife was Glenys Roberts, the journalist, and they had a daughter, Polly, who took over the tailoring business in 2006.

He made every one of my suits until the end of his working life. After he had a stroke that brought on vascular dementia, I helped him and dealt with his accountant to keep the business afloat for some more years. He died in a hospice in Mayfair in 2008, aged seventy-three. He had always been an agnostic, but received the last rites from a Catholic priest. His daughter Polly commented: 'Typical jammy bastard – gets forgiven all his sins right at the end!'

He is greatly missed by everyone who knew him.

Douglas Frederick Cornelius Hayward, tailor.

Born 5 October 1934, died 26 April 2008.

RIP

CHAPTER SEVEN

GOLF

Golf is one of those games that takes you over ... and it did me, for many years.

When I was young I got hooked, and used to play whenever and wherever I could. I practised in the garden, when the children were small, and then it escalated. Soon I was playing twice a week at Hartsbourne Golf Club, and getting better and better at the game – which naturally meant that my keenness increased.

Hartsbourne, in Bushey Heath, was essentially a Jewish golf club. When a member died there was always an obituary in the *Jewish Chronicle*. I have recently learnt that Yiddish is a language on the endangered list; well, we – at Hartsbourne – did our bit to keep it in circulation!

Hartsbourne was owned by Joe Stillitz. He ran a major clothing company called Gor-Ray and was rich and successful, but this, unfortunately, didn't make him a charmer. I eventually became Club Chairman, which gave me the 'privilege' of playing with him regularly.

I tried to help the club along. Together with a good golfer, Pat Matthews, I established a magazine named *Golfing at Hartsbourne* and ran articles entitled 'A Fashion Expert Looks at Golf', one called 'Snags at the Top' by Louis Stanley, and one by myself titled 'On Jet Snobbery' which talks about my flying for business, and describes my flight on the first 707 to New York in 1959. It also has a photograph of Clare and Joe Stillitz on their wedding day thirty years earlier, and congratulates them on their anniversary.

I really let myself go on a supplement for *Golfing Magazine* and convinced them that, if they agreed to print it, it would help everyone – increase their circulation and really put Hartsbourne on the map. I am not sure that is exactly what happened, but it didn't really do them any harm.

Joe was – shall I say – an acquired taste, but I acquired it, and he liked me too. I was therefore given the benefit of his emphatic opinions about the club and its members.

I listened to his resentment for about nine months – how they were all ungrateful people who were always trying to get something for nothing – until one day I couldn't stop myself:

'Listen, Joe,' I said, 'you are driving yourself mad. You hate the members and the members are beginning to hate you. How about giving your blood pressure a break? Why don't you step down and sell the club to the members? You will have a much happier life – and so will everyone else!'

This went down rather badly.

'They haven't got the money, and they won't be able to afford it' was the main theme of his objection.

'Why don't you sell it to me then?' I said. 'How much would you want for it?'

Silence. He looked into the middle distance, and then turned to give me a long, hard look.

'One hundred thousand – fifty thousand down, and the rest over the next three years.'

He knew – and I knew – that this was a lot of money in those days. Nonetheless, I looked back at him and said: 'OK, I'll see what I can do.'

But Joe remained very tricky; I canvassed the members – including Leslie Porter of Tesco (who was Club Captain) and Harold Raiher (Vice President). Many of the members jumped at the chance of owning such a nice place, and relieving themselves of the onerous presence of Joe, so the money was made available, and so – more importantly – was the enthusiasm. About 75 per cent of the members paid up within two weeks, so I went back to him – ready to cement the sale.

'I've changed my mind,' he growled. We had a terrible row, but his mind stayed changed, and after a while I gave up as it was obvious that it was never going to happen.

However, by now I had members willing – and able – to put up a considerable amount of cash, and we all wanted somewhere we could play, with an atmosphere that wasn't heavy with Joe's resentment and thoroughgoing dislike. With the idea firmly lodged in my head I therefore looked around for a few months, and eventually discovered Dyrham Park in Barnet, Hertfordshire.

Gita and I went down to visit it, together with our children, in 1961. It was – and still is – a wonderful large old house situated in about 200 acres. Initially an Elizabethan house (until it was damaged by fire) it is now a Palladian villa, with a sweeping staircase and minstrels' gallery. Its penultimate private owner was John Trotter, an army contractor whose family held it for four generations until it was sold.

The property was for sale at a cost of £75,000. But Leslie Porter and Harold Raiher helped me negotiate this price down to £52,000. We called a meeting of potential subscribers, and the show got on the road. We set up a committee which met every few weeks, mainly at each other's houses. I became Chairman of the Committee, with Leslie and Harold being the other two Officers and fellow Trustees, and Shirley Porter (Leslie's wife) acting as Secretary. We worked for pleasure and the needs of the community, rather than for any sort of recognition. It took about two years to bring our project to fruition, with the official opening taking place on 10 October 1964.

We appointed a greenkeeper – Ken Eastwood – whom we knew from Hartsbourne. He was a gentle, silent, good golfing giant, and he and his wife, Josie, lived in a cottage on the course, where they could keep an eye on everything.

We wanted to stock the lakes with fish, to have an indoor golf clinic, a good practice ground, tennis courts and a swimming pool – as well as a good kitchen. The automatic watering system at Dyrham inspired me to install a similar one (admittedly on a smaller scale) at my home.

We were looking for a good Teaching Pro and Tournament Pro. Some of the people we approached – Dai Rees, John Jacobs and Bill Large – went elsewhere, but we had Pat Keene as a good all-rounder and Malcolm Gregson as a Tournament Pro. Bill Large came back in 1982 and I remember that we also looked at a very young Nick Faldo who worked with us part time for a year or so.

I have only one major complaint. When I was at Hartsbourne I won a lot of competitions, including the Marquess of Lorne trophy. However, at Dyrham either my luck or my skill failed me, as I won nothing at all there, except for the Herts Alliance together with Bill Large in 1968.

I was involved with the club for five years or so, firstly as Chairman from 1962 to 1965, and then as President from 1965 to 1966. I worked hard to get the whole project off the ground, and played there devotedly for some time. However, I took more of a back seat as I began building up my business and had other calls on my time.

I have a letter from Harold Raiher, dated May 1966, which says:

> I am sorry that, for the moment anyway, you have chosen to move to the sidelines. I can only hope – with the very deep interest that I know you have in the club – that you will shortly be able to move back into the centre of things.

Meanwhile, to keep fit, having reduced my golfing hours, I played table tennis every Sunday morning with a former England international, which was terrific fun.

My interest in golf as a social emollient, an excellent networking opportunity and a jolly good day out (I disagree with Mark Twain's oft-quoted opinion that it is a good walk spoiled) continued even after I left Dyrham Park.

In the 1980s and early 1990s I used my interest in golf to set up the Conservative Party Golf Tournament Charitable Trust, with the aim of giving the proceeds to a range of deserving charities by organising a number of one-day golf tournaments for the Conservative Party. These took place in the magnificent surroundings of Moor Park Golf Club in Hertfordshire and were great days out.

We were fortunate to have the support of Sir Denis Thatcher,

Freddie Trueman, Ronnie Corbett, Jimmy Tarbuck, Emlyn Hughes, Mike Gatting, Geoff Boycott, Henry Cooper, Errol Brown and many others at these events and they were hugely popular.

Jimmy Tarbuck, Ronnie Corbett and other golfers; Lord Feldman and Denis Thatcher
at Moor Park

The main fundraising was done by way of black tie dinners held at such venues as Apsley House (the Duke of Wellington's old home) and at the Savoy – the money raised given to the selected charities at a series of receptions held at No. 10 and No. 11 Downing Street.

John Major with SCAR reps and celebrities at No. 10 (Frank Bruno, Garth Crooks)

Baroness Thatcher, when Prime Minister, was always hugely supportive of these events and one occasion stands out clearly in my memory.

We had arranged to buy an electric wheelchair for a little boy who had the Duchenne form of muscular dystrophy. He was a very bright child and was so excited that – at last – he would be able to keep up with his playground friends. The sadness, however, was our knowledge that he probably only had a few more years to live before this dreadful disease took its toll on him.

His parents were rather overawed by the fact that they were at an event at No. 10 – and even more overawed at meeting the PM. She, on the other hand, demonstrated the kindness that she was often not given adequate credit for. She took time, in a very busy evening, to take the father on a tour of No. 10 – pointing out the portraits of former Prime Ministers which lined the main staircase – and generally doing all she could to make him feel at ease.

Black tie dinner at Apsley House (l–r: Ronnie Corbett, Adam Faith, Geoffrey Leigh, Lord Feldman, Tony Jacklin, Denis Thatcher, Nigel Lawson, Therese Lawson, Trevor Brooking)

Nigel Lawson was also hugely supportive of my events and was an extremely generous host whenever I called on the use of No. 11 for such charitable receptions.

They were very good days.

In 1988 I went down to Dyrham to celebrate its Silver Jubilee, and met some of the old and new members. I was pleased to see how remarkably beautiful it still is – a proper country club and a place for the whole family, with a swimming pool, a fishing pond, tennis courts, the lot.

In April 2013 I received a letter from Ronnie Gottlieb (the president of the club) inviting me to come to celebrate the Golden Jubilee, which was due to take place at the end of June. My eldest son, Nick, came with me, and there were 325 members and their partners present, many of whom I recognised – much to my delight!

Ronnie had asked if I would give the opening speech, which gave me the opportunity of enjoying a wonderful trip down Memory Lane. It also gave me the chance to look around the club and grounds once more, and to notice the improvements that have taken place in recent years.

It is amazing to think that fifty years have gone by since I first saw the club, and I have to say I am rather proud of my part in setting it up, and when I am feeling irritated with myself I think how wonderful it would have been if I had bought it as a family home, rather than as a golf club.

Dyrham Park

CHAPTER EIGHT

TRAVELLING

One of the things that made my life exciting – apart from developing my business and putting my cascade of ideas into practice – was travelling. Not many people did it in the early 1950s; planes would take off from Croydon Airport and the whole thing was very glamorous and slightly nerve-racking, especially for those who were left behind. I remember my whole family coming to see me off, I suppose just in case it was the last time they clapped eyes on me!

At London Airport

I travelled all over the world; India was, and still is, a favourite of mine. I bought and sold materials there, and went all over the country, doing business with all sorts of people. One fairly gruelling trip was three weeks long, and I had been hither and thither, negotiating with my clients (with my heart slightly in my mouth, as I was not always convinced that I would be paid, on time or at all) and arranging to deliver the plastics they ordered. Although there was often a wait that was rather longer than it could have been, they always paid up in the end.

India, at the Taj Mahal

At the end of the three weeks, I decided to take a couple of days R&R, as I was very tired. I was sitting one afternoon on the terrace of a hotel that looked out on to an enormous beach. Music was playing and there was dancing, and I heard someone calling to me from below.

'Sahib, I tell your fortune.'

'OK,' I said to the little man standing on the sand below me, 'come up.'

'I cannot, Sahib. You must come down.'

He was an Untouchable, I realised, which made it impossible for him to come into the hotel, so I went down the wooden staircase to join him. He took my hand, and looked at it for a little while before saying – to my great amazement – 'You have a wife at home called Gita.'

After three weeks away from home, I had been missing her a good deal but I don't know how on earth he could have known. I don't think I heard anything very much after that, and have always hoped that none of my hosts had primed him with information. I somehow doubt it.

Ever since that time I have always had a very open mind about such things as fortune telling, astrology and so on.

In Hong Kong, I did good business involving glittering bales of silk and brocade, some of which I brought home and spread out in our hall so that it looked like Aladdin's Cave. I also bought many very beautiful pieces of jade, which we still have in the drawing room. I loved the food there, and enjoyed my relationships with the Chinese. I had been warned that things were not always as they seemed, so I got in first, and told them that if they conned me in any way, I would make it my business to tell everyone I knew, so I suggested they looked after me. They did!

I went to New York on the very first passenger jet flight out of London – a Boeing 707, which reached New York in seven hours and twenty minutes. This is not very different to the flying times of today, although we had to stop to refuel in Newfoundland after four hours and forty-five minutes. The trip was exciting and the novelty was increased by the fact that I was sleeping next to the scented and somnolent glamour of Zsa Zsa Gabor. There was a separate lounge for First Class passengers and, once on board, if you ordered a roast meal, they would carve the joint on a board between the seats. The return journey was even faster. With a helpful tail wind, we flew non-stop to London in five hours and fifty-five minutes! And that was in 1959.

Another business trip took me to Hungary, during a time of political unrest, and I remember being surprised when several women turned up to talk to me in my hotel room, all proposing marriage most enthusiastically, so that they could get out of the country. Although some of them were very pretty, and all seemed extremely keen, I obviously turned down their offers, and returned – rather thankfully – to my own lovely wife in London. I thought I wasn't short of problems!

In the 1950s, I visited a factory in Israel that was producing plastic sheeting which they arranged over the crops they were growing on kibbutzes. These were the first polytunnels, and the crops they were covering were melons ('ogens' in Hebrew). I invested a bit of money in the project, but didn't take any profit because I wanted to help the settlers.

Alex recalls:

They sent melons every year, and once, in 1971, when you were on holiday, a box arrived, and Stevie and I had to eat the lot! And the Indians sent delicious mangoes too – they were wonderful.

Israel had become a State in 1948, and I put a little money into various projects there, so I had a lively connection with the country. They were delightful people, artists and all sorts. It was a pleasure visiting them and doing business. I had previously visited Israel in the late 1940s on my own because I had heard that some of my mother's family had emigrated there, escaping from the Nazis. I went into the house in which they were living, and saw on the walls pictures of my mother's family. It was terribly emotional to see them living in such difficult and rather impoverished surroundings, and although I left money with them to help with their situation it was still very hard for me to witness.

Our honeymoon – 1952

I was working all the time, and loving it. In fact, even part of my rather lengthy six-week honeymoon was spent wheeling and dealing!

Our wedding

After our wedding ceremony at the synagogue and a wonderful party at the Savoy, Gita and I spent two nights at the hotel before sailing for New York on the *Queen Mary*.

We were in America for the Eisenhower election, and the party invitations came in thick and fast to my father's family, the Zellers, whom we accompanied with alacrity. We visited my uncle Ben, my father's brother, and met the Feldman family circle of about 200 people, which rather impressed me by their numbers and their support for each other.

After leaving the US en route to South America, our first stop was Trinidad to refuel, and we spent about three days there on the empty and beautiful beaches which were perfect in every way – except for the vicious clouds of sandflies which descended on Gita and feasted on her blood. We then travelled on to Puerto Rico and then to Rio, where we spent two weeks.

Our overnight flight to Rio was in a Stratocruiser, where we were swung, soothingly, to sleep in beds that hung from the ceiling of the plane. A bed was where the luggage rack is today, and you had to climb a ladder to reach it.

Brazil then was exceedingly poor. There were buildings being put up with no girders, scaffolding was rudimentary and Brasilia and São Paolo were still in the process of being built. Indeed, there was a real contrast between the old and new Brazil – with Brasilia, in particular, being at the forefront of cutting-edge architecture.

It was all very foreign to us; we saw convicts exercising on the empty Copacabana Beach, wearing their ball and chain, and if men were not weighed down with these, they played football on the sand. They were light, nimble and dextrous, and incredibly impressive. We went to see a match at the famous Maracanã stadium and were bowled over! We had thought till then that Arsenal was the tops, but my goodness, we soon changed our minds! I would have loved to have been able to get the Brazilians over to teach Arsenal a thing or two…

The scent of gardenias, Gita's favourite flower, hung in the humid air, and Sugar Loaf Mountain rose above the city into the bright blue skies.

While there, I did some business with a family who put in a very large order. They were falling over themselves to sign the deal, which was good, even though I did wonder a bit at their enthusiasm. What I didn't know was that at that time it was very difficult to get money out of Brazil, but I found out soon enough when I got back to England. It took me more than two years to be paid, but we got it in the end.

Next stop, Argentina; Eva Perón had just died, and the country was heavy with grief. All the bridges we drove over or under had her name painted on them in big letters. I bought Gita a beautiful aquamarine ring to remember our visit, which, alas, was stolen from her many years later.

Our honeymoon

After Uruguay, I asked Gita, 'Shall we go on to Peru?' – but no, she had had enough and wanted to go home. Our return journey took us via Portugal where I visited my agent, Fritz Lowenthal, who had a cut-glass German accent and a yearning for some good Jewish food.

He had left Germany to escape the Nazis, and pined for some of the home cooking he had been used to. I went back several times – each time bringing some of my mother's home cooking. She was proud to have been an important contributor to the export indus-try! Fritz wasn't impressed by the Portuguese he worked with: 'Zey know nossing,' he told me.

Years later Ladislao Winter, Fritz's senior partner, wrote me a letter, (sadly Fritz had died at this time) on hearing of my knighthood:

Dear Basil

This was – and is – the biggest sensation of the century! At least, no doubt, for us of the old times when orders of '20 quids" value were considered a success and the cost of a barrel of oil was a dollar or so. What a pity Fritz Lowenthal could not take part in this 'happening'.

Because to some extent, we of the old guard are all participating in your steep career, just as old friends of, let us say, Disraeli (or Gladstone, to avoid insisting always on the Jewish circles) might have felt when the old chum became Prime Minister. By the way, what else can be expected of you after this start?

When you mentioned your intention of entering politics I won-dered what could come out of it, although Machiavellic booklet for the right strategy of publicity in favour of the Conservative Party gave already proof both of your ambitious plans and of your capac-ity to work miracles in that field. But if you had been appointed

Minister of Commerce, it would have been somewhat less amazing, because I always associate 'Sir' with some pompous gentlemen like the Earl of Avon, Sir Anthony Eden or similar classical British figures.

In earnest, what are you planning now? What is the Conservative Party planning now? I mean, in view of the by jerks growing socialistic tendencies in the world? I am myself rather a monarchist, in spite of Habsburg's no end of failures, but the wheel of history can hardly be turned backwards. Well since you are now nearer to God, or at least to Downing Street 10, you might have a solution at hand...

I shall have to take the first opportunity of a Fair in England to congratulate you personally and to see how Basil Feldman of old days looks in the guise of Sir Basil.

We mixed with the great and the good while we were in Portugal. The Conde de Cabral was a friend of Gita's father, and his son Jacinto met us at the airport in his sleek sports car, which was recognised and ushered on at traffic lights by the policemen in their white gloves. The family owned Perugina chocolates, the bulls used in the bullfights, and led luxurious lives. I do recall the parties were very glamorous and plentiful.

My father wrote me a long letter from America, while he was there on one of his trips in 1969:

We checked into the Beverley Hilton and were given a lovely room. It really is the best room we have had, including the last trip – spacious, comfortable, plenty of wardrobe space – even a colour television if you want it. The entrance to this hotel has been changed and so have some of the dining rooms, but it is still a lovely hotel.

Its population – or residents – comprise many nationalities. One hears and sees Japanese, Chinese, Mexicans, coloured gentry who we did not see last time and all in all there is a coming and going constantly.

He talks of going to Disneyland and Vegas, although with regret cancels the Grand Canyon trip. They hired a Lincoln Continental with a 'chatty and very helpful driver' who got them a special guide when they reached Disneyland, where they had lunch in a Tahitian restaurant.

He mentions various relatives, and describes a visit to the Hollywood Bowl, and then dinner with Rene Falber and her family – 'very nostalgic atmosphere; she had three grandchildren – the eldest Debby is quite a lovely spark, and only three and a half!'

Next they flew to San Jose, and on to Stockton to see Ben Feldman – his brother – then on to Washington, back to New York, and then home. While in New York, they went to see *Plaza Suite* and also a musical – *Promises* – 'a must when it gets to London. It has been running for about 7–9 months and it is very difficult to get seats, but we managed.'

Of course they did! Another Feldman – Jerry – invited them to a wedding in Maplewood and arranged transport for them to get there.

I was delighted to read these letters from my father, and to feel that I was able to send him and my mother to see relations in

America and to have such a good time. Family matters a great deal to the Feldmans!

Holidays

My travelling was by no means confined to business, although somehow I always found time for a little, wherever we were. Once we had a family we enjoyed many trips together.

Italy was a family favourite. We loved Venice, especially Nick, who was quite literally speechless at the sight of the red sky at dusk on the Grand Canal. I remember, in Positano, we sat on our balcony overlooking the deep blue sea below, and there on the next balcony, doing much the same thing, was Ernest Hemingway!

We enjoyed the remoteness of Ischia, but getting back to the mainland was a different story. The hydrofoil to Naples was delayed and we had the Rome Express train to catch. Disembarking, I hailed two taxis and tipped the drivers generously to get us to the station. We hurtled along, our luggage on the roofs, the children and Nanny in one car, Gita and I in the other, being flung from side to side as the drivers outdid each other skittering down narrow streets (probably the wrong way), turning sharply with a screech of tyres and a smell of burning rubber… Gita and I arrived at the station by the skin of our teeth, but there was no sign of the others. Disaster! I rushed to the platform and to the front of the train, and another generous tip, this time to the driver and the guard, ensured that Mussolini's train timekeeping, for once, was not perfect. My children remember this whole escapade vividly to this day!

After we had checked into the hotel in Rome, I was so exhausted by all the bribing and rushing about, I walked flat bang into a plate-glass window and spent the rest of the holiday with a plaster on my nose. This has, of course, been ruthlessly recorded in all the family photographs, and still causes much hilarity when the photo albums come out.

France was another joy. We liked going south and stayed at the Carlton in Cannes, and rented a house in the hills above, near Vence.

Gita recalls:

I met Elizabeth Taylor at La Reserve in Beaulieu in the South of France. She was unbelievably beautiful, and utterly charming. Someone came up to her table while she was eating her dinner and asked for an autograph, and she was very nice to them, and to everyone else.

In the mid-60s, we went to Biarritz where we stayed in a hotel on the beach. And lo, next door were the Duke and Duchess of Windsor, she wearing eye-popping jewels right up her neck, he quieter and content to be in her company. Rather oddly, he wore galoshes when he went swimming in the pool! They were visited constantly, and the parties bubbled almost without cease. We weren't invited, of course, but one of their guests, Sally Crichton-Stuart, who became the Begum Aga Khan, liked the children, so we saw a bit of her.

Barbados

We started going to Barbados about forty years ago, and stayed at Sandy Lane, a charming hotel, owned by the Fortes. We loved it – it was exclusive but very quiet and unflashy.

Gita remembers:

The Fortes lived directly opposite us in Hampstead with their large brood. Their son Rocco would come home very late in a large, throaty sports car. Their house was very grand, with Canalettos hanging on the walls. One of my uncles – a cabinet maker – put up his father, Charles's, first ice cream bar in Bournemouth!

Some years ago the hotel was sold, and then rebuilt. Hence the atmosphere changed a bit, and now we stay at the Royal Pavilion, but still drop into Sandy Lane for dinner quite often.

We made a lot of friends in Barbados and John Cleese was one of them. I remember him and his then wife Alyce Faye sitting on sunbeds next to each other, reading the same book, so they would be able to discuss it.

John was either very funny or very depressed. He can be very serious and you can have long talks with him. When he met Robin Skynner, with whom he wrote *Families and How to Survive Them*, he found someone who understood and supported him, a father, really. Skynner worked with one of my tutors, who married Jonathan Lynn, and we used to meet John at parties there too.

New Year Party at Sandy Lane

Gita remembers:

Basil introduced me to Hugh Grant, who is a very intelligent man, but all he wanted to talk about was his girlfriend Elizabeth!

Michael Caine is delicious. He gave me a lovely greeting kiss one day, and I have always thought that it can only go downhill from there. He did a marvellous imitation of Harry Secombe being a Goon, while Harry was in the back of the same car, laughing his head off.

One day Michael Winner told us that we were all going to be in the film he was finishing off. Jenny Seagrove, then Michael's girlfriend, was there (we love her) and so was Roger Moore (one of the most charming people you could ever meet) and he photographed us all on the beach, lying in deckchairs and when the titles roll at the end we are all there in the far background!

Mick Jagger had a house on the island, and took his family there often. Before he had children, we were startled when we landed in London, after some weeks in Barbados, and his wife Bianca was allowed on the plane to look for him. He was not on the plane as we knew very well, having seen him the day before on holiday with Jerry Hall, who was about to leave her then beau, Bryan Ferry – Ferry also had a house in Barbados. Years later we met Bianca at dinner – Gita sat next to her and they talked about her humanitarian work. She is doing wonderful things, but poor Gita delved deeply for her sense of humour, and came up empty handed.

We met Gerard Mortier, the Belgian who ran the Belgian Opera at La Monnaie, before he went to Salzburg to run the Festival there.

We became quite friendly with Edward Heath whom we introduced to interesting people who were also staying at the hotel. He became a regular and we would visit him at Arundels, his house in Salisbury. He introduced us to Pappano, another Salzburg conductor, who invited us to the ceremony when he was given an honour by the Italians. Contrary to his reputation, we found Ted interesting, amusing, very clever of course, and excellent company.

CHAPTER NINE

SALZBURG

I went to Austria for the first time in 1966 – initially to Vienna, to look at sheeting products. This was good business, but this first visit started a passion for Austria that Gita and I have had ever since.

I remember on this first visit being met at the airport by a rather well-fed man wearing lederhosen and a hat with a feather, who had been sent to meet us by the Schmidberger Werke factory at Wels, near Salzburg.

How charming, I thought, he has put on national dress to welcome us to his country. However, it soon became clear that he was wearing what he would wear every day – just like most of the other men around him. At the end of this visit – and as I was driving back to the airport from Wels, in order to get my flight back to the UK – my companion (an Austrian from the company we had been doing business with) waxed lyrical about a hotel called the Sacher. It sounded so nice that I decided to stay for the night – and she was right, so right that when I told Gita about it, we decided we would return there, and travel to Austria much more regularly in future.

Some years later – and on another business trip – I decided that I would travel back to London via Salzburg, and would stay for the night at the Hotel Schloss Fuschl, which had been recommended to me as an interesting place to stay.

The hotel was built in 1461 for the Prince-Archbishop of Salzburg, Sigmund I. It was a hunting lodge for 300 years, and then owned by a fascinating collection of people – including a master mariner, a pair of hotelier brothers, several aristocratic families, industrialists such as the Thyssens – and also, for a short time, it was requisitioned by the Nazis and transferred to von Ribbentrop, who moved in with some alacrity in the summer of 1939.

Schloss Fuschl, in the 1950s

When the Americans approached at the end of the war, von Ribbentrop had the contents of his splendid wine cellar sunk into the lake – and some bottles are still occasionally discovered even today by scuba divers enjoying the depths of its fresh water. There were other rumours of gold bars and coins also having been hidden in the woods and the water, but nothing has been found of any great note to date.

The Schloss Fuschl became a hotel in 1947, and was very popular with the international glitterati. Visitors have included Nehru and his daughter, Indira, Jean-Paul Sartre, Ava Gardner, Audrey Hepburn, Peter Ustinov, Yul Brynner and all manner of international statesmen. The hotel was much smaller then than it is nowadays, and our room – Room 7 – wasn't all that great. Nevertheless ever since our first visit Gita and I have returned each year in August, and staying for about three weeks on each occasion. We time our visits to coincide with the Salzburg Festival, and normally try to fit in at least ten Festival performances on each visit.

We always request the same room – which has been improved enormously over the years. Prince Charles also tends to favour this room for his visits but recently the hotel (very flatteringly) held him off until we had confirmed the dates of our visit!

Our room has sometimes had other guests apart from ourselves. One day we were woken by the gentle scuffling of dormice (*Siebenschläfer*) who were happily nibbling away at the Mozartkugeln which had been left on our pillows... The management ensured the mice were gone by our next visit, but we enjoyed them while they were there.

Over the years we have continued to spread the word about the hotel, and several of our friends have visited including Tim Rice, the late Richard Colburn (an American philanthropist, and long-time friend), Ted Heath, and my greatest success – Margaret Thatcher – whom I convinced to stay at the Schloss instead of going to Switzerland as she usually did.

I suggested that it might be a good pace for her to meet and talk to the crowned heads and political figures of Europe, with no publicity; advice that proved to be extremely useful. Margaret came to the Festival for five years running, and one year she also used the Schloss to chair a meeting of European political leaders, where they discussed European and world affairs.

I remember one occasion when she was enthusiastically welcomed to the hotel by a brass band which was gathered at the entrance, all oompahing merrily while the rain poured down. An umbrella was respectfully held over her head while she listened to the music and her bouffant hairdo slowly drooped in the rain – something she serenely ignored.

Gita grew up with classical music – her father being a pianist – and I love listening to both opera and orchestral music. We have also been fortunate enough to enjoy amazing jazz in Salzburg, including performances by Artie Shaw and Stan Getz.

As a result of our great love for Salzburg, and also for the Festival, I was asked if I would become Chairman of the Salzburg Festival Trust in London – which was formed with the aim of encouraging new audiences to Salzburg at the time of the Festival each year. Trustees included Laurence Watt, Martin Campbell-White and Jeremy Isaacs.

Friends of the Salzburg Festival paid £500 annual membership, and were invited to meet performers and also attend an annual reception – hosted by the Austrian Ambassador – at the Embassy in London.

I ran this organisation for several years, and in 2003 I was given the Silver Decoration of Honour by the Governor, Dr Franz Schausberger, in honour of the work that I had done.

Silver Medal of Honour

Basil, Gita and Salzburg Governor, Dr Franz Schausberger

Eight members of the Vienna Philharmonic Orchestra were also honoured on this same occasion and as this is one of our favourite orchestras, it made the occasion even more special.

Basil and Gita with members of the Vienna Philharmonic

A little while later I stood down as Chairman – a position which was subsequently taken up by the American philanthropist Donald Kahn.

Gita and I really love the Salzburg area – the beauty and surroundings of the Schloss, and having the opportunity to relax and listen to wonderful music. I remember that in the early days the dinner menu at the Schloss was about thirty pages long, and the wine list was extensive and excellent.

The Schloss has now gone through another phase of development; the castle itself remains externally the same, but inside it has been transformed. The rest of the hotel has also been completely rebuilt – as has the seating plan around the lake.

We hope to continue to visit the Schloss – and Salzburg – for many years to come, as it provides everything we love and need for a holiday – a comfortable hotel in beautiful surroundings, good service and good food.

We also enjoy the fact that we have the chance – weather permitting – to swim in the lake during the day, and then go into Salzburg at night to listen to great music and opera at the Festival.

Many of our friends come from all around the world to visit the hotel at the same time as we do each year, and so we have the chance to find out what has been happening in one another's lives.

Basil and Gita with Nora and Peter Wiegmann

CHAPTER TEN

BETTER MADE IN BRITAIN

In 1978 I got a telephone call from Denis Healey, then Chancellor of the Exchequer.

'Hello, Feldman,' came those unmistakable tones so beloved of Mike Yarwood. 'I hear you're a man of ideas, and I wanted to ask you something...'

'Can I tell you my biggest idea?' I asked him. 'I'm Chairman of the Conservative Party in London, and my main aim is to get rid of your lot at the next Election!'

He laughed, and said, 'You'll never be able to do that,' and then went on to tell me that he wanted me to be Chairman of the Clothing Economic Development Committee. This was what people in the industry called a 'Little Neddy' and was an important part of NEDO – the National Economic Development Office.

'As long as I've told you my plans,' I replied, 'I am prepared to consider your proposal. I have to say, however, that I know nothing about the clothing industry – although I do like wearing nice clothes!'

It was extremely unusual for the Labour Party to approach a Tory – especially a dyed-in-the wool Tory like me, but Healey was no fool; this was a business decision, not a political one, and he had heard that I could be good at what he wanted me to do – which was to cut the imports of clothing to the UK, and provide employment for the local workforce. At the time the industry was in real trouble, mainly because of the growth in imports, and the general decline of manufacturing industry in the UK.

After spending some time on the new committee, and after I felt that I had got to grips with the industry and with the Unions, I felt that we should do something different. After many meetings – and much 'sweet talk' – I managed to convince the committee that I should organise what I came to call a 'back to front' exhibition.

Until now, suppliers always tried to sell their wares to retail buyers – but we decided to do it the other way round by introducing buyers from the various stores to British companies who could produce what they were importing from other countries. This had never been done before, and it was a real breakthrough for a lot of people.

Baroness Thatcher arriving at the Clothing Exhibition

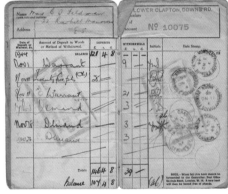

ABOVE LEFT Basil aged four

ABOVE RIGHT Basil aged eight

BELOW LEFT Basil as a pageboy at Aunt Laura's wedding

BELOW RIGHT My Post Office savings book!

Gita's father, with Coral, Gita and Helene   Waiting to board the flight to Rome

Basil and Gita – so happy and so much in love

ABOVE LEFT
Basil and Gita with the children

ABOVE RIGHT
With Alex, aged four

MIDDLE LEFT
My beautiful daughter, Alex

MIDDLE RIGHT
Nick in the early Wang
Chung days

BELOW
Steve with his wife, Andi

Philomena, Maximilian, Jessica and Gabriella

My Dad, with Steve, Fenella, Alex and Nick

At Moor Park with Freddie Trueman, Eric Sykes and Henry Cooper

With Denis Thatcher, Tom King and other celebrities at Moor Park

At Moor Park for the Conservative National Golf Tournament, October 1986. L-R: Donald Stringer, Sheila, Basil, Robin Nelder's secretary and Robin Nelder

Sharing a joke with Tony Jacklin, Golf Tournament Dinner, Apsley House, 7 November 1985

Nigel Lawson and celebrities at No. 11 for the Conservative National Golf Tournament Reception in 1987 (Ronnie Corbett, Garth Crookes, Bob Monkhouse, Bernie Winters, Duncan Goodhew, Sue Pollard, Tim Rice)

Sir John and Dame Norma Major with celebrities at No. 10 for the Conservative National Golf Tournament Reception in the late 1980s

With Baroness Thatcher, Impact Campaign Dinner, Army and Navy Club, 21 October 1982

End of a Party Conference: Mayor of Blackpool, Basil, Gita, Jim Hodkinson (B&Q), Baroness Thatcher and Denis Thatcher

Two of the National Union Area Chairmen, Hazel Byford and David Kelly, presenting me with a gift on my retirement as National Union Chairman

With Sir John Major outside Conservative Central Office

With Sir John Major and National Union Chairmen

10 DOWNING STREET

THE PRIME MINISTER

Dear Sir David,

    I welcome the "Better Made in Britain" Exhibition which is
to be held in London on 16 and 17 March.

    This is the first Exhibition of its kind and I wish
it every success. I hope that similar exhibitions will be held
in other parts of the country.

    I hope that, wherever United Kingdom manufacturers can
match foreign goods in design, price, quality and delivery dates,
retailers will choose British goods.

    I am encouraged that there has been so much enthusiasm from
retailers and manufacturers for this Exhibition.

    I hope that the Exhibition will seek to make a reality of
the words which you have chosen - "Better made in Britain".

Yours sincerely

Margaret Thatcher

Sir Basil Feldman.

Letter of congratulations from Baroness Thatcher

Our first exhibition – in 1983 – was centred on clothing. We had
twenty-two exhibitors who collectively represented 60 per cent of
high street clothing sales, and between them they showed 2,000
imported items which they would prefer to source at home –
providing they were commercially competitive. Two hundred

manufacturers came to meet the buyers on the various stands, in order to try and win back the work for their factories here in the UK.

Let our consultants help you

Experienced consultants (known as Ambassadors) with special knowledge of the respective industries are available, without charge, to discuss the prospects of the industry and the work programme and recommendations of their sector committees at joint meetings arranged on company premises. The consultants are able to indicate where further advice and assistance may be obtained.

Sir Basil Feldman shows the Princess of Wales around the exhibition. In addition to attendance by many people of vital importance to the apparel industry, letters of support were received from over 80 VIPs including the Prime Minister, trade union leaders and senior industrialists.

With Princess Diana at our first BMIB Exhibition in 1983

The exhibition was opened by Princess Diana (which was quite a coup and did our profile no harm at all!). After she had made her opening remarks we presented her with a tiny T-shirt for William, printed with the words 'Better Made in Britain' and which she accepted graciously. I had written her a letter asking if she would be prepared to come along and help get the show on the road, and she didn't hesitate. She was completely delightful, and very funny.

One of the events planned during the course of the exhibition was a lingerie fashion show. Diana sat next to Gita to watch the models parading up and down, and at one point she leaned over and whispered in Gita's ear: 'People have a go at me for being thin, but look at this lot – not a decent pair of tits between them!'

The whole thing was very successful, I am delighted to say. Word soon got about, and plenty of other companies were happy to be involved in subsequent exhibitions. One particular success story was that of Stuart Mensley, Knitwear – who were amongst our early exhibitors. After the first clothing exhibition they went on to do £1.1 million worth of business with C&A – where their products replaced items being sourced in Italy and the Far East. They next targeted Asda, and that brought about a further quarter of a million pounds' worth of business – once again replacing imports.

BMIB published *Briefing* – a regular journal covering all the different industries; it was distributed to supporters and all those interested in our work to date.

In my Chairman's message, I wrote:

The Better Made in Britain exhibition has established an unique Blueprint for a new form of cooperation between retailer and manufacturer. As a result of the 1983 exhibition, £20 million worth of previously imported clothing is now being made in British factories. Our expectation for the second exhibition is that a further £100 million of clothing, knitwear and footwear will be made here by the end of 1986, and thousands of jobs – both directly and indirectly – will be created or saved. Better Made in Britain is a simple but practical concept. There is something positive in it for the retailer, the manufacturer and the consumer. It is not based on patriotic exhortation, but on sound commercial criteria. So where do we go from here? Into many other industries is the answer … We have already been approached to do this – and we will. Import substitution – which is what Better Made in Britain is all about – has the capacity to create or save tens of thousands of jobs in the UK, by providing closer cooperation between retailer and manufacturer, and between manufacturer and manufacturer. So let us continue working together on a commercial basis, and fully develop this opportunity of playing a practical part in strengthening British industry, and in reducing unemployment. Britain can make it. It is – indeed – Better Made in Britain!

Mr P Peters of BHS shows a garment he would prefer to buy from a British manufacturer to Sir Basil Feldman and Mr Len Murray, TUC General Secretary.

Why buy in Britain?

Patriotism is not enough. "Buy British" by exhortation is a very short-lived event – there have to be sound commercial criteria for buying from British manufacturers. This was the clear message that leading retailers gave at the exhibition. But by their very participation at the show these same retailers gave ample evidence of their desire to seek British merchandise of the quality and price they require.

Comments picked up at the show also underlined this desire . . .

"Our policy on sourcing goods is to buy the right goods at the right price to meet our specifications for quality clothes from whichever suppliers are most reliable. We prefer to work with

"The majority of merchandise we sell is sourced in this country, and we have been trying to increase this percentage with some success since our Great British Value promotion some years ago." DEBENHAMS.

"Quality and price are vital with our clothing merchandise, but our preference for British goods is supported by our consideration, where appropriate, to allow a 10% premium in price for getting a domestic-made product." ASDA

"We try to buy merchandise in order to pass on to the customer the best in styling, taste and value. And if this comes from abroad, then we will buy from abroad. But, of course, if the British

With Len Murray, TUC Chairman, and Mr Peters from BHS at one of our clothing exhibitions

With Princess Diana, at the opening of our 1983 exhibition

The format of our first clothing exhibition was repeated for other industry sectors. Between 1983 and 1987 three large-scale exhibitions and one, more specialised, version covered clothing, knitwear, footwear, home furnishing, lighting, carpets, furniture and textiles. In the spring of 1987 two more exhibitions were planned – repeating the successful formula for clothing, knitwear and footwear – and breaking new ground with DIY, building products and hardware.

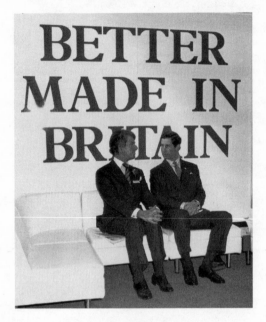

Chatting with Prince Charles

Prior to our exhibition – which took place on 9 April 1987 – the Prince of Wales very kindly hosted a reception for Better Made in Britain, which took place at Lancaster House.

At the reception he congratulated me on the effort I had put into the campaign and on the success we had achieved so far, and exhorted the 200 leading businessmen present to greater effort.

John Davis of *The Observer* wrote in his investment column:

As Prince Charles stressed in his eloquent address, the scope to do more is enormous. He ended his speech by asking Feldman to let him know what new converts had been made. One whom I know was sufficiently moved was Stanley Kalms, the Chief Executive of Dixons Group. 'I think it is an excellent idea, and I will see what we can do to help' he told me. Prominent amongst those already championing Feldman's cause is Sir Philip Harris. 'In the past year alone we have re-sourced back to UK manufacturers an additional £4 million of goods we had previously bought abroad'. More is the pity, therefore, that there is no way yet open for investors to invest in Better Made in Britain – for this looks to be a grown situation par excellence.

Mrs Thatcher opened the exhibition the next day and – as always – was full of praise for our efforts in trying to cut imports and to meet the challenges that faced us.

Baroness Thatcher, cutting the cake at our building exhibition in 1987

Brian James, of *The Times*, wrote:

Does it say 'Made in Britain'? This is a most uncommon event – a sales jamboree made back to front; that is to say, instead of makers coming to display their wares, the big retailers who dominate Britain's high streets decked out stands with goods which they had imported, and asked British manufacturers 'Why can't you make us something like this, at something like the price?' Sir Basil Feldman, the patriotic zealot who is Chairman of the campaign, easily finds the figures to explain the need. 'Nearly 35 per cent of all the manufactured items used in our homes and factories are purchased abroad. Our shops are jammed with products we ought to set our own people to make for ourselves and to sell to the world,' he said. And there is no excuse that will satisfy Mr Peter Rogers – Construction Director of Rosehaugh Stanhope plc (the company masterminding the Broadgate development in the City of London). He estimates that, of the £500 million building cost some £170 million in purchasing will go abroad – which makes him seethe. He said, 'My company will never buy abroad from choice. Yet time and again we have no option – either because our native technology is not up to the work – but much more often because British companies simply will not accept the risk inherent in investing their time on big projects. We wanted British lifts throughout the development. We even gave a home company a deliberate edge on the pricing – but they pulled out. Too much for them; so Germany will install our lifts.'

It was predicted that by the summer of 1987 Better Made in Britain would have brought back about £100 million worth of business to UK manufacturers – saving, or creating, approximately 7,000 jobs.

Stuart Mensley said:

Business from Better Made in Britain has played a significant part in
the growth and profitability of the company over the last four years, with
turnover growing from £1.8 million to £5 million in 1985/6. This additional
business, alone, has enabled us to take on forty-five new employees, as well
as to acquire a further knitwear company with a workforce of 160 people
– many of whom may otherwise have faced redundancy.

The Economist wrote: 'Sir Basil Feldman – incoming Chairman of
the National Union of Conservative Associations – seems to have
persuaded half the Government to become involved with his brain-
child, the Better Made in Britain Exhibition.'

Mrs Thatcher, in a speech to the 1985 Conservative Conference in
Bournemouth, was also very enthusiastic:

If a British-made product is as good as the foreign-made one, then
Buy British. Very often it can be 'Better Made in Britain' – and Basil
Feldman, here on the platform, has done much to prove just that.
Let's give every encouragement to those who want to set up a new
business. They can be the biggest job creators of them all.

Prince Charles was also a great supporter. He came to several exhibitions,
and asked to be sent regular updates of our work. In June 1987 – when
addressing a meeting of Enterprise Agencies – he said of Better Made
in Britain: 'A remarkable group of people slaving away with very small
numbers of staff – and they have a very good idea of doing an exhibition
in reverse. I thought it was a particularly effective exhibition.'

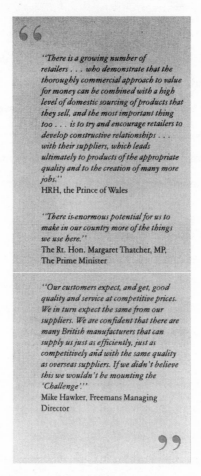

"There is a growing number of retailers . . . who demonstrate that the thoroughly commercial approach to value for money can be combined with a high level of domestic sourcing of products that they sell, and the most important thing too . . . is to try and encourage retailers to develop constructive relationships . . . with their suppliers, which leads ultimately to products of the appropriate quality and to the creation of many more jobs."
HRH, the Prince of Wales

"There is enormous potential for us to make in our country more of the things we use here."
The Rt. Hon. Margaret Thatcher, MP,
The Prime Minister

"Our customers expect, and get, good quality and service at competitive prices. We in turn expect the same from our suppliers. We are confident that there are many British manufacturers that can supply us just as efficiently, just as competitively and with the same quality as overseas suppliers. If we didn't believe this we wouldn't be mounting the 'Challenge'."
Mike Hawker, Freemans Managing
Director

Extracts from speeches made by the Prince of Wales, Baroness Thatcher and Mike Hawker, MD of Freemans

I have met Prince Charles many times over the years, and he is always open, friendly and amusing. When Gita and I, together with her sister, Coral, were walking through the Chelsea Flower Show one year we bumped into him. He greeted me with a broad smile and the words, 'Hello, Basil, have you got any new ideas for me today?'

As a result of the contacts I had made during the first clothing exhibition, I got to know many of the department store heads, and also their designers – and we worked together to see if we could find some way of bringing designer fashion to the High Street in a more economical way. During this time I worked closely with the British Fashion Council, and others – and in 1987 'Designers at Debenhams' was born.

This was the first diffusion fashion range established in any High Street store – with the designers being Jeff Banks, Jasper Conran and John Rocha – who were later joined by Betty Jackson, Ben de Lisi and Julien MacDonald. This idea of carrying a diffusion range has since spread to other stores and other sectors of the market, and continues to attract customers and flourish.

Jasper Conran, a great supporter of British products and manufacture, told the press, 'The quality of workmanship in Britain is superb.'

Prince Anne cutting the cake at our 1991 food exhibition

Princess Anne opened two later Better Made in Britain exhibitions, and I particularly recall the exhibition we held in 1991 for the food and drink industry. After cutting a splendid cake we had had made for the occasion she said, 'This is a very pertinent and worth-while exhibition, which fills a desperate need to make connections. Quality is much more important than quantity in this instance, and when you say "*Better* Made in Britain" it is not just "Made in Britain" – it must mean precisely that.'

The *Express* opined:

Sir Basil Feldman – rightly – laments that 70 items capable of being grown here are being imported. Eight out of ten apples sold in our shops are not home-grown and the same goes for tomatoes. His reason is that British suppliers cannot provide the right quality, consistency or price – so France, Germany and Holland prosper, while Britain's balance of trade is undermined. It is time for a new initiative on the whole vital question of import substitution. Clearly some heads need banging together to demonstrate that Britain Can Grow It!

Daily Express *editorial, 22 February 1991*

With chefs at the 1991 food exhibition

In the spring of 1986 I organised a seminar to be held at Downing Street, and chaired by Mrs Thatcher. The idea behind this seminar was to launch a national campaign which would stress the quality of British goods.

Leading figures from Government and Industry who were present on that occasion welcomed our initiative – but underlined the importance of supporting the campaign with an authoritative endorsement of the quality of the goods concerned, rather than relying on simple appeals to patriotism.

We went on to form a Steering Group which was comprised of major industry heavyweights such as John Banham, Director General of the CBI; George Davies, Chairman of Next; Sir Philip Harris, Chairman of Harris Queensway; John Poppleton, Public Affairs Executive of Marks & Spencer; Geoffrey Samson, Managing

Director of Hotpoint and many more – and so the Quality Mark was born.

Our idea was to show – by means of a swing ticket attached to goods in varying sectors – that these goods had a guarantee of quality. We agreed that the base standard we would use would be that of BS 5750 – the British quality control systems standard – and wanted to encourage people to purchase items showing our 'Quality Mark' logo as they could then be assured that they could not only source goods here in the UK, but that they would be of a superior quality to those offered elsewhere.

There were other ideas, too, which we hoped would boost UK jobs and cut imports.

Following on from the various Better Made in Britain exhibitions, we identified a number of areas in the UK where there was high unemployment, and where we could – perhaps – audit the components that local industry sectors were importing to run their businesses, and once again see if we could 'plug the gap'.

We called this programme REGAIN – and planned it to work as a partnership between the local business support agencies active in the area, such as Business Link, Tec, Chambers of Commerce, the Enterprise Agency and the local authority EDUs. Close sponsorship and support from large local industry was also sought, especially for help in promoting the programme.

We initially concentrated our efforts in three areas – Kirklees, the West Midlands and Tyneside. The results were astonishing. In Kirklees alone, our audits of local companies discovered that they were currently importing £102 million worth of raw materials and

components – and the Directors and Purchasing Managers interviewed thought that it should be possible to source 75 per cent of
these items in the UK.

THE REGAIN PROGRAMME: *Recovering lost markets*
The Exhibitions have highlighted the high degree of imports in components. The REGAIN
programme will quantify these opportunities on a regional and/or industry basis. Researchers will
carefully survey areas of high unemployment. Data on imports obtained will form a presentation
of opportunities in the region: and businesses will be encouraged to manufacture for these market
gaps.
　　Information provided will be available for a National Database. The programme starts in
summer 1987.

THE QUEST PROGRAMME: *Promoting endorsed British Quality*
The penetration of so many British markets by imports has happened over a number of years. It
coincided with a decline in our national reputation as manufacturers of quality products. We
welcome the growing realisation of the central importance of quality improvement to our
industrial recovery. The QUEST programme is designed to accelerate the regeneration of quality
manufacture, endorse consumer products that reach nationally agreed standards with a single
authoritative label, and to promote the concept to retailers and consumers.
　　It is crucial to success that retailers and consumers have confidence in the quality and value
of the products associated with it. To achieve this, the programme will require objective criteria
ensuring that the products are using nationally accepted quality standards, and are tested by
recognized bodies.
　　The QUEST initiative lies at the heart of the BMIB plan. A Steering Group drawn from
industry and the public sector will formally launch the programme in the early summer. The
launching of industry sector schemes will begin in the autumn, leading to the National
Advertising and Promotion Launch to retailers and consumers in the course of 1988.

THE EXHIBITION PROGRAMME: *Widening the possibilities*
The high profile retailer/manufacturer exhibition programme has proven to be an effective way of
presenting the commercial opportunities identified by retailers. A full calendar of exhibitions
will therefore form the backbone of BMIB's communication with industry. The exhibition
programme is likely to develop in two ways. National exhibitions run in conjunction with NEDO
will re-enforce the message in industries where a bridgehead has been established, and bring in
industries not yet exposed to the technique. Regionally, exhibitions are likely to be tailored to the
region or industry concerned, and may be sponsored by a local organisation.

REGAIN plan of attack

In Lincoln, Andrew Rouston – the inventor of Bluebird Screw Ties
for builders – told us, 'We have only been manufacturing for six
months and already have a £250,000 turnover. I expect that to be
half a million next year – but we are now working to capacity.'

Marconi also expressed their preference for working with local
firms, saying, 'It is much easier to deal with them face to face, and
this is very important in business.'

Structured training programmes for unemployed people with experience of business were developed and this REGAIN work provided excellent opportunities to gain new skills, or refresh old ones – and also helped them make new contacts within the local business community, which inevitably led to jobs.

Better Made in Britain sought to establish good relationships with the main organisations with whom it was working. We kept in close contact with the CBI and the TUC – and kept them firmly in the loop, encouraging their input to programmes as they developed.

They saw that I was doing valuable work towards job creation and I built up excellent working relationships with the Trade Unions – which surprised many people, who rather expected them to be the flies in the BMIB ointment!

At a Better Made in Britain dinner in 1986, Chancellor Nigel Lawson spoke warmly and positively about our successes and also about the future for British retailing: 'I was particularly struck by Sir Basil's estimate that an extra £75 million worth of goods are now being produced in British factories – a figure which is expected to rise to £100 million early next year.'

He went on to cite the example of Harris Queensway, 'Which placed business worth more than £4 million – including substituting a British carpet supplier for a foreign one'.

He concluded his speech, saying it was vital that Government and business – and business and business – all worked together.

Apart from our Better Made in Britain exhibitions, we also organised what we termed 'Challenge Days' with retailers – usually on the opening of a new store.

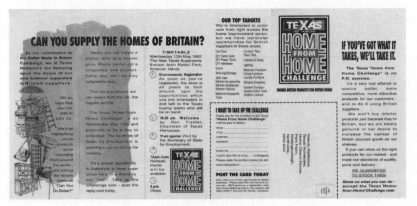

Literature from Texas Challenge Day, May 1992

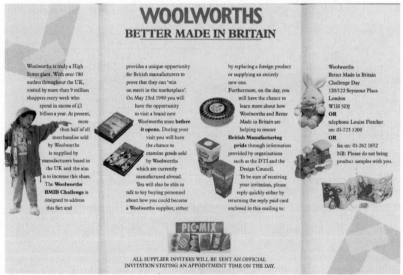

Promotional material from Woolworth Challenge Day, May 1990

B&Q Challenge Day literature from 1987 and 1988

Literature from the Freemans Open Day at QE11 Conference Centre, 6 February 1990

In 1987 B&Q invited manufacturers to visit their new store in Leigh, Lancashire – and as a result of this more than £6 million worth of business was won back to Britain.

Baroness Thatcher making a purchase at the 1988 B&Q Challenge Day

This was followed – just as successfully – by Texas Challenge Days in 1992 and 1993 at their stores in Andover (visited by Gillian Shephard, then Secretary of State for Employment) and at Huntingdon and Ayr in Scotland.

The Andover event made it possible for sixty-two new accounts to be opened – more than half for entirely new ones, and the rest for existing suppliers, who were able to supply a wider range of other goods.

The Huntingdon Challenge Day was opened on 24 September 1993 by the Prime Minister, John Major. As Chief Secretary to the Treasury he had already been guest of honour at a very successful Challenge Day organised by Halfords in 1988, and he carried his enthusiasm for Better Made in Britain with him.

There were several hundred representatives of manufacturing

companies from all over the country, and the entire Texas buying team was present throughout the day – talking to buyers and making appointments to meet in the future. For the first time we specifically invited both UK and EC suppliers.

Other companies who joined in to make the most of the Challenge Days were Woolworths, Next and Freemans. Challenge Days had stands which made it possible for visitors to get expert advice. The Better Made in Britain stand would be joined by a Department of Employment, Training and Enterprise stand – and there might also be one, for example, giving information on packaging design.

In September 1988 Better Made in Britain celebrated its first five years by holding a birthday party at the House of Lords – which was hosted by Lord Aldington and myself. Guests included interested Peers, and the Chief Executives of manufacturing companies and leading retailers – many of whom had been BMIB exhibitors.

When we launched Better Made in Britain in 1983 Lord Jenkin – then Secretary of State for Industry – had backed our work, and in an impromptu speech at the party he said, 'Better Made in Britain's achievement has convinced even the most cynical that change can be brought about, and that market share can be won back for Britain by determination and flair.'

Successful though BMIB was – and this is undeniable, as it is one of the projects that I have organised that I am most proud of – it wasn't all plain sailing.

To carry on Better Made in Britain's good work I founded the Construction Industry Working Group, with a twelve-strong board consisting of various industry heavyweights. These included Godfrey

Bradman of Rosehaugh, Stuart Lipton of Stanhope (a very successful 1980s property company that, alas, is no more), Lord Taylor of
Taylor Woodrow, John Fletcher of Trafalgar House, Neville Simms
of Tarmac, Frank Lampl of Bovis, Alan Cockshaw of AMEC, Pat
Jackson of Rugby, Sir Jack Zunz of Ove Arup, Jim Hodkinson of
B&Q and Michael Coates of Gardiner and Theobald, the worldwide construction company.

An article written at the time by Andrew Pring fairly accurately
highlighted the odds that were stacked against me. Although Pring
starts by saying how impressed he is at what he calls 'this illustrious
team' he was – like others – cautious about its success, saying:

Set this year to counter last year's staggering £2.5 billion plus annual
trade deficit in building materials, its chances of turning a commercial tidal wave appear negligible at best. However to dismiss Sir
Basil as a modern day Don Quixote battling naively against a world
he does not understand is to misunderstand badly the man and his
aims. The 61-year old former Tory Party Conference Chairman –
whose contacts across the political and commercial spectrum are
legendary – is a shrewd entrepreneur with proven business acumen.
A hard-bitten realist, Sir Basil knows the art of the possible, and
has more modest ambitions than he is often labelled with. Of the
hard economic decisions home producers must make to justify their
investment, he is cool and level-headed. Such experiences will need
to be multiplied many times over for any real impact to register. But
those who know Sir Basil will not be surprised if his group's influ-
ence begins to spread. The qualities that have won Mrs Thatcher's

admiration – persistence, commitment, fighting spirit – are now allied with the authority carried by Construction's senior statesmen. It offers a formidable combination and arguments that become more compelling the nearer 1992 draws – even for the cynic.

I told Pring that I saw my role as maintaining the consciousness-raising. I had started with BMIB. I wasn't interested in promoting protectionist policies – a buyer and seller partnership was the point. I wanted them not to be against each other in the ring, but to work together and to keep Britain's manufacturing alive by giving it somewhere to go. If the commercial basis was sensible – and the purchaser could see this – then there would be no point in going abroad for something that could be made in this country, competitively priced and what they needed.

When Mrs Thatcher opened our 1987 exhibition for building products and DIY she was – she said – shocked to see how many of the items on display were produced abroad. At the time Michael Howard – then junior trade minister in Tokyo – was doing his utmost to ensure the best trade deal for Britain – but as Mrs Thatcher said at the time, 'More freedom was still needed.'

I was consequently asked – by the Government – to head up a special visit to the Far East and also to encourage investment into Northern Ireland.

I had spent a considerable amount of time working together with the Northern Ireland Development Board members who were keen to attract manufacturing industry to the Province. We had been working for more than a year trying to convince Japanese banks to visit Northern Ireland, and consider inward investment – and

finally in June 1990 I headed up the largest ever visit to Northern
Ireland of leading Japanese companies and bankers.

I was helped in this task by James, Duke of Abercorn, who was
based in Northern Ireland and also by Richard Needham, then
Under-Secretary of State for Northern Ireland – who was present
to meet the Japanese visitors and who hosted a dinner for them at
Stormont Castle during their two-day visit.

Report of the visit to Northern Ireland in June 1990

With His Grace the Duke of Abercorn, Sir Richard Needham MP and members of Sumitomo Bank, on their visit to the Province

The visit did much to give hope to the struggling Northern Irish economy, and Chris Buckland – Chief Political Editor of the *Daily Express* – said at the time, 'The two-day visit was hailed as a triumph. It came after a year of patient negotiations to persuade the Japanese that Ulster isn't all bombs and bigotry. Within hours of their arrival, it was revealed that Sumitomo Heavy Industries wanted to set up a joint venture, bringing hundreds more jobs to the region.'

Yoichi Abe, General Manager of Sumitomo, said, 'This is the first time I have been to Northern Ireland. Now I wish I had come before. I shall certainly advise clients to set up operations here.'

In an article in *The Times*, Jimmy Burns outlined the formidable task of attracting investment into Northern Ireland:

The first wave of Japanese investment in the UK in the early 1970s coincided with Northern Ireland's 'Troubles'. The Japanese invested in Wales, Scotland and the Republic of Ireland, but their presence in the Province has been limited. Some Japanese investment has begun to be channelled into Northern Ireland in the last five years – but of the 150 Japanese manufacturing companies operating in the UK, only four are in the Province – employing a total of 2,500 workers. Leading the Japanese mission to Northern Ireland is Mr Yoichi Abe, General Manager of the Sumitomo Bank in London.

'Our biggest concern is security,' he says. 'In Japan our executives look at TV and see bombings. My wife is worried that I'm on this trip. We can't understand this religious war.' On the London/Belfast shuttle the party settles down to read the glossy package of briefing notes provided by the Industrial Development Board (IDB). Information ranges from the number of championship golf courses on offer, to the availability of Government-backed financial incentives and large numbers of young skilled and semi-skilled workers who rarely strike.

Mr Tim McNeill, the Board's Asia-Pacific Director, says of the Japanese, 'They want to feel welcome, they want people who are committed to their work, they want a healthy lifestyle – and yes, they want to feel safe.'

An article in *The Economist* – under the heading of 'Ulster Sushi' - said:

Given the choice between a more familiar kind of kamikaze mission and a posting to Belfast, most Japanese businessmen would probably opt for a quick course of solo flying! Japan's television coverage of the Province – the usual diet of bombs and burials – has long implied that even the most honourable salary man set down in Northern

Ireland is likely to be murdered in his bed. So it was something of a coup for the Province's Industrial Development Board that it managed to lure over a dozen senior Japanese managers on 2 June, to assess the risk for themselves.

The IDB had spent months fixing up the trip, with the help of the London office of Sumitomo Bank – whose senior Director, Mr Yoji Okabe, once spent a holiday motoring safely around the Ulster coast. The visitors were left in no doubt that (as an IDB executive put it) the murder rate is lower in Northern Ireland than in Denmark, or Anchorage, Alaska.

The itinerary included stops at a couple of Japanese-owned factories, where the local managers duly said 'no, they had never had any security worries' – but 'yes, the labour costs were incredibly low'. Northern Ireland's first Japanese restaurant served up sushi in Newtonabbey, which seemed to impress the party almost as much as the information that there are fourteen golf courses in the immediate vicinity of Stormont alone!

And an irrepressible Mr Richard Needham – Minister for the Economy – led them on a sightseeing tour of Belfast that wound up with a dinner in their honour in Stormont's Parliamentary buildings. This produced the most dangerous encounter of the day ... with a seafood platter that had probably seen better (i.e. pre-Direct Rule) days! The evening finished with visitors and hosts all coming together to sing 'Danny Boy' with enough spirit to rival the Mitsubishi Heavy Industries male voice choir.

But do Ulstermen have anything to fear from the Japanese? Ask the local businessman in Newtonabbey, who took a knife and fork to his first plate of sushi. He set off across the plate with laudable resolve, only to swallow his entire blob of (highly explosive) Japanese mustard in one go. 'This has nothing to do with emotion' he whispered through his tears.

Mr Okabe later wrote to Richard Needham, saying, 'All that remains for me to say is that after the visit we all feel very much encouraged with regards to investment in Northern Ireland, and that we wish to continue to further develop our already good existing relationship.'

Richard Needham and I later travelled together to the Far East to continue our mission to sell British goods – this time abroad.

With Sir Richars Needham and others in Japan

To sum up, Better Made in Britain organised twenty-five major exhibitions covering fourteen different industry sectors, and brought back more than £2 billion worth of business to British companies – saving, or creating, thousands of jobs.

Much work was also done in the construction industry to bring buyers and sellers together.

We developed twenty REGAIN programmes in towns all around the country, and successful smaller exhibitions were also held to bring business back to a particular town or city.

The government today is thinking once more along the same lines as we did with BMIB – although they are calling it 'Made in Britain'.

In February 2010 Lord Sanderson of Bowden moved a debate in the Lords on the subject of Economy, Enterprise and Innovation. Lord Wade of Chorlton – amongst others – voiced many Peers' concerns by saying that the debate represented 'one of the most important matters that we can discuss. We are now in the most competitive world that we will ever see. If we do not get down to wealth creation, the economy of this country is doomed to be even worse than it is now.'

After a response from Lord Sugar – predictably about apprenticeships and enterprise schemes – I had the opportunity to talk of my own experience, the concept of which I believe could be adopted to be of use again today.

I spoke of my Better Made in Britain experience – talking about the twenty-five different exhibitions that we had run, and of the benefits they had brought to both manufacturers and retailers alike. I reminded them, too, of our work in Northern Ireland, and also said that:

We established the Quality Mark, which was a standard of excellence in manufactured goods, based on the British Standard Kitemark.

I believe that these concepts could be updated and used today, and that the Government should appoint the right person to organise it. Times are difficult, and jobs are being lost on a daily basis, so I hope that this concept (or a version of it) will be considered positively, as I have experience of it being successful.

Lord Hunt of Wirral took this up, mentioning, 'My noble friends, Lord Wade and Lord Feldman, remembered business incubation units – so many ideas exist.'

Lord Davies of Abersoch supported 'the comments made by the noble Lord, Lord Feldman, on the fashion industry. They highlight the facts that exhibitions are hugely important for a range of industries.'

Better Made in Britain became very important to the trade – and to the country. It was demanding work, but I enjoyed the challenge, and above all – I delivered. It wasn't easy; I worked all hours of the day, every day, going into work five days a week, and spending the other two dreaming up ideas. It would have been more sensible to spend time making money, some would say, but I don't regret a moment!

The successes of Better Made in Britain have never yet been repeated – mainly due to the economic firefighting which continues within successive Governments. We can but live in hope!

CHAPTER ELEVEN

THE ARTS IN LONDON

February and March are historically the quietest months for London theatre.

As we all know, this is generally a rather flat time to visit London. The weather is usually cold, wet and depressing, which can lead to empty seats in theatres and empty rooms in galleries echoing to the sound of one or two pairs of heels walking on the parquet past a somnolent guard. However, as an enthusiastic Briton, Londoner and also someone who cares deeply for the performing arts, I decided to do something about this.

I had been a member of the English Tourist Board since 1986, and had a plan to bring together London's theatre, music, entertainment and art venues – and to market them using the British Tourist Authority offices worldwide.

It was logical – I thought – to link tourism and the arts – particularly emphasising London's unique position as a centre for arts and entertainment, and so I set about convincing the English Tourist Board, the London Tourist Board and the British Tourist Authority that this idea could work.

It wasn't easy to get off the ground, with years of rejection, and it took sheer obstinacy on my part to get it up and running. It took a while to put together my ideas, and then another year to get people to agree to let me develop them. However, it finally took off and ran, successfully, for three years.

Joanna Coles, in a *Guardian* Commentary in February 1994, has said that I 'deserved an award for plugging away at it for so long. It has taken Feldman twelve years to persuade arts organisations to cooperate with such a scheme.'

She went on to remind people that

> Feldman has met considerable resistance to his suggestion. He met it first in 1986, when he suggested it over poached salmon at a special dinner for leading figures in the arts world. He met it again, four years later, when he proposed it over roast saddle of lamb.

She was right; the National Operas, National Theatre and the Arts Council all claimed that London was too big and didn't need such a thing. Eventually, they began to realise that perhaps it did. However, once we managed to get the ball rolling, we all worked our socks off to bring together more than 100 venues in London, and to offer the widest possible choice of events (more than 300) to visitors.

We launched our London Arts Season in September 1993, with a cocktail reception at the Hyde Park Hotel, and this was followed early in 1994, when Prime Minister John Major hosted a VIP reception at Lancaster House, which was attended by some 350 celebrities, many MPs, Ambassadors, cultural attachés and representatives of the arts and of tourism.

Sir Basil Feldman

on behalf of
English Tourist Board
British Tourist Authority
and London Tourist Board

invites you to the launch of
LONDON ARTS SEASON 1994
a major new promotion of
the capital's arts and entertainment

on
Tuesday 28th September 1993
11.30 am for 12 noon
at
The Hyde Park Hotel
Ballroom Entrance
66 Knightsbridge, London SW1

RSVP
Joanne Oliver, THP
45 Islington Park Street
London N1 1QB
Telephone 071 226 7450
Fax 071 359 6026

11.30am *coffee*
12 noon *presentation*
12.30pm *champagne and canapes*

Invitation to the launch of London Arts Season, 1994

Gita recalls:

I watched Felicity Kendal and Judi Dench chatting away – they were both tiny! Basil presented Prince Charles with two mini polo sticks – one for each of the little princes. I always enjoyed the Arts Seasons – I would tell Basil whom I would like to meet, and 'hey presto' he would invite them.

At the opening dinner I sat next to Isaiah Berlin, and listened to his wonderful voice that seemed to come up from his boots! We also became friends with Yehudi Menuhin as a result of the Arts Seasons, and dined with him at his house in Highgate.

Through the British Tourist Authority offices, we marketed the

London Arts Season in twenty-seven countries, encouraging people to book in advance, and making it very easy for them to do so. A 24-hour booking line was set up and operated via the London Arts Information Centre (open seven days a week) and by local agents in twelve countries.

The Arts Season was a really good example of public and private organisations collaborating; we were sponsored by Andersen Consulting, Forte Hotels and by Visa International.

The *Sunday Times* and Superchannel were our media sponsors, and the Foundation for Sport and the Arts, the Society of West End Theatres, the London Arts Board and the Arts Council were all involved.

Our first London Arts Season took place in 1994, and on 8 February in that year Dame Diana Rigg and Tom Conti turned on the lights illuminating the central tree-lined avenue of Park Lane, which was specially floodlit by Westminster Council in our honour. London began to hum; theatres were busy, galleries were full of visitors and people were really beginning to understand why London was such a wonderful place to come for culture and the arts.

José Carreras, Anne-Sophie Mutter, Jessye Norman, André Previn and Sir Georg Solti were the first Season's classical attractions. Picasso's paintings were exhibited at the Tate, and Fabergé artefacts on show at the V&A. There were theatreland walks and celebrity parties, and we made it possible for people to get tickets to sold-out musicals such as *Phantom of the Opera* and *Sunset Boulevard*.

In all, some £20 million worth of additional income was

generated for London (through hotels, restaurants, retail outlets, taxis etc.), with almost 43,000 tickets sold at arts events, and 100,000 specific enquiries handled.

Visitors came from all over the world, with significant numbers coming from the USA, Canada and Europe (and especially from Germany).

The first London Arts Season was such a success that we committed ourselves to producing further Arts Seasons each February and March until 1996. The English Tourist Board also undertook to fund new arts seasons in 1995 in Birmingham, Bristol, Manchester, Southampton and Yorkshire.

In planning for our second Arts Season we sought to widen the attractions for prospective visitors. Accommodation and travel packages were put together so that people could book everything at the same time, and we also devised exclusive events including behind-the-scenes visits, and private viewings.

A free London Arts Card entitled holders to discounts and special offers at arts venues and restaurants during February and March, and a White Card was a cost-saving season ticket to thirteen museums and galleries.

The number of extra attractions increased each year. For example, an Open House Weekend was launched, when twenty of London's arts venues opened their doors for a look behind the scenes, for the princely sum of £10.

'1995 is the year to be in Britain,' I told my audience, at the press launch of the Festival of Arts and Culture, which took place at the Savoy Hotel in November 1994.

Front page of brochure for 1995 Festival of Arts and Culture

A blockbuster of a campaign – a massive achievement – a celebration of the arts throughout the UK. Working together with the English Tourist Board, the three other National Boards and the Regional Tourist Boards, the British Tourist Authority have spared no money, spared no energy, spared no manpower, and spared no marketing skill in order to promote this Festival all over the world.

It was a glittering occasion, attended by the Secretary of State for National Heritage, Stephen Dorrell MP, the conductor Neville Marriner, and a host of actors and other arts luminaries including Tom Conti, Jenny Seagrove, Margaret Tyzack, Paula Wilcox and Martin Jarvis, to name just a few. We were serenaded by the three girls from *Fascinating Aida*, and I well remember having my photograph taken with members of the cast from the musical, *Cats*.

With Stephen Dorrell MP, Neville Marriner, Tom Conti and members of

Fascinating Aida, *Savoy Hotel, 1995*

English Tourist Board members 'strut their stuff'!

With performers from Cats

As part of our plan to launch the Festival of Arts and Culture, I had written to a number of leading figures from music, theatre, film, fine art and television asking if they would agree to become Ambassadors for the Arts Season, and give it their support and seal of approval. I had not one refusal and ended up with a list of seventy people – starting with Jane Asher and Alan Ayckbourn CBE, and finishing with Sir Peter Ustinov CBE and Penelope Wilton.

In 1995 John Major once again agreed to be the host at a reception at No. 10 which celebrated the second year of the London Arts Season, and the start of the 1995 Festival of Arts and Culture throughout Great Britain.

With Sir John Major at the launch of London Arts Season

No. 10 reception, 1995, with Hugh Grant, Dame Judi Dench,
Nigel Hawthorne and Michael Williams

One hundred and eighty guests attended this reception, including many of our newly created Ambassadors – actors such as Hugh Grant and Nigel Hawthorne, Dames Diana Rigg and Judi Dench, novelist Freddie Forsyth, Sir Andrew Lloyd Webber, Joan Collins, Shirley Bassey, Michael Ball and many others.

With John Major and Shirley Bassey at No. 10

Sir John Major, with Fenella at No. 10

Looking back through the 1995 guide I see we had *Miss Saigon, Les Misérables, Sunset Boulevard* and *Blood Brothers* on the menu. Peter Hall's *Hamlet*, the Vienna Philharmonic with Bernard Haitink, a Shakespeare Day at the Globe with a tour, lunch at the Barbican, and a matinée performance of *Love's Labour's Lost*. Performances at fringe theatres such as the Old Bull Arts Centre in Barnet, the Orange Tree in Richmond, and The Gate were also on offer.

Our third Arts Season took place in 1996, with Prince Charles hosting a very special party at St James's Palace. Once again we were delighted to receive support from the great and the good of the arts world, including guests such as Sir Yehudi Menuhin, Kiri Te Kanawa, and Joan Collins.

With Prince Charles and Yehudi Menuhin at St James's Palace, 1996

Lynne Burton, the Arts Season Director, has said:

Billed as one man's dream, the London Arts Season was the brain-child of Sir Basil Feldman, who was a member of the English Tour-ist Board at the time.

He first mooted the idea of a London-wide arts festival in the mid-1980s, but was told it was inoperable. But nothing daunted, and with dogged determination, Basil worked hard to persuade the three tourist boards of the time that his idea was workable and would benefit tourism.

I worked very closely with Basil and can vouch for his enormous enthusiasm and indefatigable campaigning for this project. He man-aged to obtain massive support from four funding bodies, a range of big sponsors and top media partners.

It was certainly a mammoth task to bring together. Our small team liaised with hundreds of arts venues across London, worked with numerous ticketing agents and tour operators, over forty London restaurants and BTA offices overseas. We produced millions of detailed brochures in five languages and conducted a high-profile advertising PR campaign in twenty-seven countries.

But it wasn't just about practicalities. Basil was keen that we create some special events for the London Arts Season. We were ahead of our time, as it is only in the past few years (and especially in 2012) that major campaigns have featured this type of 'money-can't-buy' event. We were also ahead of things with the launch of the London Arts Card and provided a platform for the launch of the White Card – this was before free entry became the norm for many of these institutions.

Basil ensured that the campaigns had the highest possible profile through his many high level contacts. We launched with a starry champagne event at the Hyde Park Hotel in September 1993 and this was followed early in 1994 with an opening reception at Lancaster House with the Prime Minister John Major, who hosted ambassadors, cultural attaches and numerous glamorous stars and eminent people from all art forms. In the subsequent two years we had another splendid reception at No. 10 Downing Street and a very special party at St. James's Palace, hosted by HRH Prince Charles. Once again these events were attended by the great and the good of the arts world.

The London Arts Season was a huge success. It ran for three years, gaining in momentum and status as it went, and generated an estimated £75 million for London and its cultural venues.

Sadly it came to an end in 1996 as the funding was no longer available. However it was a catalyst for many permanent schemes, as well as other campaigns – and thanks to Basil, firmly established the London cultural scene as the best in the world.

When I first had my idea to organise a London Arts Season, I was struck by how little those working in the arts seemed to know each other, and that it was really important that they should.

People had never thought of doing it before – and arts, culture and tourism (for me such obvious bedfellows) had never been that close.

They had kept themselves to themselves, and had not explored the exciting possibilities of working together to spread the word about London's wonderful arts offerings.

For two months of the year, in 1994, 1995 and 1996, we managed
it. And I live in hope that one day it will happen again.

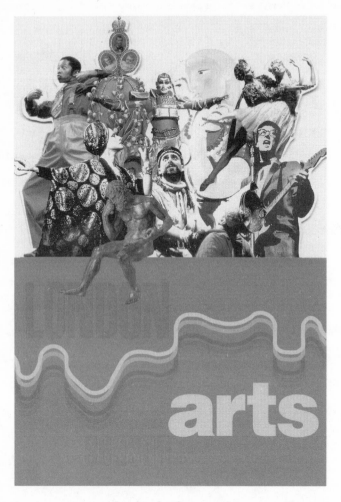

London Arts Season card

CHAPTER TWELVE

STARTING OUT IN POLITICS

By 1972 I was thinking more and more about going into politics. I was forty-nine, and I had been successful in business for many years, learning a lot and working hard. I was already interested in politics, which I suppose I define as using my skills to get things done for the good of the country. The Conservative Party seemed the right place for me and I began to get more involved.

The Richmond by-election, 1973

I was already associated with the Conservative Party, and on the Candidates' List, but as there were no major elections on the horizon, I was in limbo; waiting and hoping for something interesting to come up. Suddenly something did...

Raine Spencer, then Lady Lewisham, had been the representative of the Conservative Association on the Greater London Council Housing Committee in Richmond for nine years. She had now decided that the time had come for her to bow out, and did so, three months before the election. She left an old-fashioned Party that was pretty stuck in its ways, and I saw this as the opportunity to put some of my own ideas into practice, although it was clear that the Liberals were the front runners.

With Raine (Countess) Spencer

Gita was amazed when I came home and told her that I had decided to run for the newly created Richmond vacancy – I had always been interested and she knew that, but this was one step further. Undeterred by the unlikelihood of winning, I girded my loins and was invited to interview. I accepted, of course, but told them I could come only after a planned business trip of three weeks to the United States.

The British approach

When I returned from the States, I put on one of Doug Hayward's suits and went to be interviewed by a roomful of tweedy ladies in pearls, and some old army gentlemen, wearing their own uniform of creased suits and unpolished shoes. It was not the thing in the

Joan Collins at the London Arts Season Reception

BELOW Simon Callow and Diana Rigg at the LAS Reception

Greeting David
Puttnam at the Arts
Season Reception
at No. 10

Shirley Bassey
and Joan Collins
sharing a joke,
LAS Reception

With performers at
the Festival of Arts
and Culture launch,
November 1994

With David Seaman
and Bob Wilson
(Arsenal) at the Fresh
Hope Trust
Reception,
St Stephen's Club
December 2009

Recipients of cheques
given at Fresh Hope
Trust reception,
St Stephen's Club,
December 2009

With members of the Renaissance Forum, July 2010

Basil and Gita, Salzburg
Festival 2005

At Salzburg, with our
good friend Richard
Colburn

ABOVE Leaving
Pflaums in Bayreuth,
on the way to the
opera

With Gita in
Barbados

New Year Party in Barbados (Basil and Gita, Michael Winner, John Cleese, Michael Caine, Harry Secombe and their respective partners)

Basil, Terry O'Neill and Michael Winner in Barbados

With Gita, on my introduction to the Lords

BELOW With the family on my introduction to the Lords, February 1996

With Phil and Pauline Harris at our first State Opening

Steve's 50th party, L-R: Basil, Gita, Steve and Andi

Party to look too smart then – you could look good in country clothes, but otherwise a good tailor was an irrelevance.

I think they had almost decided on their candidate, and it was clear they wanted a grandee. I was far too flashy and unfamiliar: suit too good, shoes too shiny, not from the shires, definitely not one of them. Indeed, someone in the Party even said that I was a bit too 'showbiz'!

Nevertheless, I pressed Central Office to get them to see me, and I was on very good form at the interview, had lots of ideas (as always!), and they decided to take a chance, especially as time was extremely short.

It did not take long for them to realise that my ideas about campaigning differed fundamentally from theirs. They believed that turning up on the day would do it, but it became clear on the doorsteps that I had no chance. Nevertheless, I was going to give it a damn good go.

A more American view

I had arranged to visit my brother-in-law – William Safire – in the United States. William, who was married to Gita's sister, Helene, was a very well-known and well-respected political journalist who had won the Pulitzer Prize in 1978. He had worked as a speechwriter for Richard Nixon, and had even been involved in the famous 'kitchen debates' between the President and Nikita Khrushchev. Even though I had already been interested, and involved in politics for many years, I was hugely grateful for his advice. Sadly William died of pancreatic cancer in 2009 – aged seventy-nine – just three years after receiving the Presidential Medal of Freedom from George W. Bush.

In particular, he showed me the value of putting the word out by using all mod cons (such as the telephone!) to reach the electorate, and try to win them over. We followed his suggestions with excellent results. Of course the Major Generals minded all that terribly. They told me that telephoning people was an intrusion, which I countered by saying that I would much rather be interrupted by a phone call which I could hang up than by some stranger standing on the doorstep sporting a rosette and waving a clipboard. They weren't sure about that, but they graciously agreed, and it shut them up for a bit.

Campaigning

Campaigning with the family in Richmond

Although many in the Party weren't too sure of my campaigning methods (which they probably thought were rather too direct), although I didn't win this election, I made my mark and the Party's campaigning was never the same again.

After two days on the doorsteps, I told them we wouldn't win, but said I would give up work to concentrate on proving myself wrong. We had lapel badges saying 'Vote for Feldman', T-shirts, boaters, umbrellas, car stickers, posters, you name it. I had brochures printed and delivered with photographs of myself and my family and the PR machine got my name and face in the local papers, sometimes with my family, looking young, dynamic and approachable. I was.

Vote for Feldman!

Meeting the locals

Campaigning on the streets of Richmond

I approached the whole thing very professionally, which also worried the ancients, who preferred to treat the Party workers like the troops. They didn't understand business, and found my approach very difficult to stomach. But it was obvious it was working. I wrote a manifesto, and I taught my team how to approach people on the telephone and in person, and generally cheered everything up. We lost, as I knew we would, but people were impressed, and I was asked to be Vice President of the Richmond Conservative Association, which of course I accepted. I became President in 1984.

My campaign document

I worked with Sir Anthony Royle, the Conservative MP for Richmond from 1976 to 1984. We got on well. A senior Party officer, he knew I wasn't fighting for his seat and was pleased that I wanted to strengthen the Party. He was a supportive ally, tall, handsome, with a good sense of humour and a sense of taking the Party forward. He died earlier than he should have done and I miss him.

With Sir Edward Heath, in Richmond

In 1975, after the hurly-burly of the Richmond election had died down, and I had been involved with the Party for a year or two, I decided I needed someone young, intelligent and hard-working to help me. To this end I placed an ad in the *Daily Telegraph*:

Right Hand Man wanted for busy company chairman. Must be interested in – and motivated by – Conservative politics.

David McDonough, who had just left Oxford, applied along with many others.

I whittled the list down to three: David, Bruce Anderson and – rather oddly, given her subsequent politics – Patricia Hewitt.

I gave them all an essay to write about 'The Greening of London', and David's submission was the one I thought the best. It made me feel that he would suit the job, that he could work with me and I could throw things at him for him to run with. This is exactly what happened.

David recalls:

I thought the subject was rather an imaginative thing to get people to write about, and I was delighted to get the job, on the strength of my effort (typed by my father's secretary!).

I was essentially Basil's private political secretary. He had ambitions for the Tory Party, and said to me, 'Together we could really get somewhere, and map out a course.'

I was twenty-two, and although I had been pretty active in Oxford University politics, this was a different kettle of fish. God knows what I knew about anything, but I gave it a go. My brief was to advise and guide, to write to the press, and work on establishing a rapport with Conservative Central Office.

I did my best. I wrote letters to the press, I wrote speeches. Basil was Deputy Chairman and then Chairman of the Greater London Area, and was out for lunches and dinners, day after day, night after night after night, to Enfield, Ealing, Kensington, Hornchurch, you name it. His sheer remorseless application and bright ideas kept him going.

Basil then decided to offer me as a resource to Margaret Thatcher's office and to members of the Shadow Cabinet. He paid my salary and I worked part time for various prominent Conservatives. When Mrs Thatcher went to the USA on her first visit as Leader of the Opposition, for example, we produced a huge briefing document for her, covering the themes of her speeches, whom she was meeting and where – that sort of thing.

Basil has always been a magnet for new ideas of policy, bringing people in, and getting money out of them fearlessly! He planned his fundraising scientifically: he started supper clubs, had dinners on subjects to which he wanted to draw policy attention; and in 1975 produced 'Constituency Campaigning', a hugely influential and still useful booklet which I worked on with him and Roger Boaden. It was all about using resources at a local level, directed at getting the Conservatives in again. I have still got my copy signed by Mrs Thatcher.

We printed some 100,000 copies and made sure that all the Constituency Associations got a copy. Margaret Thatcher was very impressed with this, and made this clear to everyone in the Party.

Mrs Thatcher became a huge fan of his. She liked his energetic

North London-ness. He would ask difficult questions, encourage people, and he would never give up.

He had about four times more energy than any other human being I ever knew!

The Richmond Conservative Association needed a leader to take them into the twentieth century, and from 1977 I worked my socks off for them. I had a loyal and efficient agent, Penny Proctor, and real support from most of the Party.

The old gentlemen harrumphed in public and sulked in private, but everyone else gave me respect and affection and things changed – for the better, it was generally felt. I was valuable to Richmond, and Richmond was certainly valuable to me: I enjoyed myself enormously. I was able to try things out, and practise my ideas to see if they worked and, if they did, to polish them until they worked even better. I made contacts, and got a taste for politics which took me on to the next level.

CHAPTER THIRTEEN

WORKING TO MODERNISE
THE PARTY

In 1975, after the Conservatives lost the Palewell and Richmond Town by-elections, and in the face of increasing Liberal popularity, I knew that our approach had to change if we were going to get back into power.

As a businessman, I brought all my experience of learning what motivates people. I made my first speech as Chairman of the Greater London Area at the Conservative Party Conference in Blackpool, in October 1977:

> In an enterprise-strangled Britain we have been stuck with a gambler's policy of double or nothing.
>
> In four miserable Socialist years, we have seen prices doubled, unemployment doubled, union power doubled, brain drain doubled, and taxes doubled, and what do we have to show for all this agony – nothing. What have they done for enterprise – nothing – and for effort and initiative – nothing. We surely have had enough of losing as a nation. Let us make Margaret Thatcher's next Government the winner we need: a Government that will encourage the wealth creators, the entrepreneurs – those takers of

risk – and not bury them like the Socialists, those undertakers of British industry.

Why does the industry need the kiss of life? We all know the reason. It is lack of incentive. Bring that down to earth and it means that all of us who work ask ourselves a simple question. That question is nothing to be ashamed of or to feel guilty about. It is at the heart of human nature. That question is: 'What's in it for me and my family?'

When there is nothing in it for the worker, nothing in it for the manager and nothing in it for the investor, then there is nothing in it for Britain.

As a businessman, I have seen incentives turn nothing into something, so I wrote to the Chancellor about incentive funds to reward managers and workers for achieving outstanding five-year targets. They are not get-rich-quick schemes. They are in the national as well as the corporate interest, and what a case-study British Leyland would make!

I appeal to Sir Keith to see that our next Government considers them. Coupled with tax cuts, I am convinced they will be the stimulus we need to put new spirit into the economy. Let us give these pacemakers of prosperity their just rewards. Britain cannot live by oil alone, and after the North Sea bubble has burst we must see that our real wealth, the talent of our people, remains the enduring foundation of our prosperity.

Despite passive and not so passive resistance from some Party members, I had to tell it as I saw it. I thought hard, and wrote *A Political Plan for Richmond and Barnes*, based on the manifesto I produced for my first attempt at being elected. It makes it clear that something has to be done, and that the situation is not a happy one.

I told the Party:

If we are frank, we must agree that in a Council election – held now – we would lose very heavily.

It won't be as easy to deal with the Liberals today, as say, five years ago, but with a mixture of hard work, political common sense, enthusiasm and money we can inspire our existing workers, bring in new ones and – over a period of one or two years – produce a dramatic and lasting improvement in the situation. We can inspire our existing dedicated workers, many of whom have devoted their lives to the Association.

It was the workers, as far as I was concerned, who made things happen, and I thought it vital to involve them and make them feel wanted.

I therefore suggested that:

We can win in the future by playing political CRICKET as follows:

- Communication – use all available techniques all the time
- Relevance – give our voluntary helpers a feeling of relevance in their work
- Identification – find out why voters have reduced their identification with us, and produce a plan to counteract this
- Campaigning – carry on political campaigning all the time
- Keenness – a strong and interesting campaign will bring renewed keenness
- Enthusiasm – to our existing and future workers
- Training – have an organised training programme for canvassers and workers, so we can maximize their work

I became Vice President of the Greater London Young Conservatives in 1975, which gave me an opportunity to put some of this into practice. These are the principles that I have applied throughout my time in the Party, and I still believe they are the best ones to follow.

They work – that's all there is to it.

Design

I have always been aware of the importance of good design; on paper, in hustings, on television. In 1982, John Butcher was appointed minister of design and technology by Mrs Thatcher, and initiated a seminar at No. 10 to consult established designers – including Michael Peters.

I had worked with Michael while I was doing Better Made in Britain in 1983, and I introduced him to Mrs Thatcher and suggested that he might like to do some design work for the Party. Michael had just one stipulation – that he work with her direct. This was agreed, and he got on with things.

There had – for many years – been a torch logo for the Conservative Party, but Mrs Thatcher wanted something new. Michael told her that if things were changed too drastically she would be in danger of throwing the baby out with the bathwater. He therefore produced various designs and eventually the torch logo, which already existed somewhere as an identity element, was decided upon. His design team worked to make it more dynamic and modern, but also gentler and more human. They also decided to add a sense of moving forward, like an Olympic flame, and added a hand.

Conservative 'torch' symbol

Peters recalls that Mrs Thatcher thought the hand rather masculine to begin with, and asked for it to be more feminine, and thus suggest that it might be hers. Peters therefore made the arm more feminine, Margaret liked it and everyone was happy.

In a later interview in the press in 2009 Michael says, 'I think she will ultimately be remembered as one of our greatest ever prime ministers, so I felt very privileged to have the chance to work with her. She was a wonderful person to work with – a very quick learner.'

The youth vote

I was very concerned about young people, and how we could involve them in the Party. They had been largely ignored up until then, and I knew that the under-25 voter was increasingly hostile to the Conservative Party – a situation we ignored at our peril.

I made it clear that many young electors found it hard to identify with the Conservatives, and as and when we became more involved with the community, we could begin to win them back.

This – as you can imagine – made the Old Guard's hair stand

173

on end, and I kept sticking it up by finishing my paper with a very clear call to arms, saying, 'We live in a world where the pace of change has increased exponentially. It therefore follows that, unless we continue to change our tactics to match the constantly moving situation, we will always have political problems.'

In 1975 I became Vice President of Greater London Area Young Conservatives (then led by Nick Robinson – who has, for many years, been an excellent BBC Political Correspondent).

I felt that these youths were an enormous fund of energy that should be tapped and motivated – and Iain Macleod (a former Chancellor of the Exchequer) obviously agreed with me, as one of the last comments he made while a member of the shadow Cabinet was to say, 'The Young Conservatives are a political youth movement which would be the envy of any political Party within the Western World.'

Nigel Fisher wrote of Macleod that 'They [the Young Conservatives] felt he was expressing their views at the highest level, and he never lost their support and loyalty. He listened to them with tolerance and respect; his idealism and humanity were an inspiration to them, and he gave them generous encouragement.

'He was certainly a man to follow!'

I had done my homework, and found that one significant factor, as far as the Conservatives were concerned, was the crumbling away of the youth vote in the last three General Elections. I considered this to be the biggest psephological time bomb ever. It was vital to find out why this was, and to do what we could to reverse the trend.

Most young people had grown up in an era when Britain was

struggling. There was a lack of awareness of popular Conservative measures – except for pensions – and the Party was generally considered remote and out of touch.

Young people – just like their parents and the rest of the community – wanted improved living standards, curbed inflation, equality of opportunity and a compassionate society. They were especially concerned with the quality of life, anti-pollution measures, free birth control, crime, health education and aid for the handicapped. Unfortunately they did not associate the Party with those ideas. My research showed me that much of what the young rejected was seen as what the Conservative Party stood for...

Meanwhile the Liberals were attracting the youth vote, and I pointed out that this was not going to change unless we improved our communications, were very careful not to patronise the young, and encouraged their involvement in the Party. They needed to be taken seriously – encouraged to become Councillors, for example – or to take Association Office, to join amenity associations – perhaps, even, to consider becoming MPs. The point was not to treat them as delivery boys.

I found out that twice as many young people listened to news on ITV than on the BBC, and that they read the *Daily Mirror*, *The Sun*, the *News of the World*, the *Sunday Mirror* and *The People* in preference to the broadsheets. Therefore, whatever our own opinions, we needed to concentrate on these – and on special interest paper and diary columns.

At Conferences I would bring on the young and the old to talk about their needs and issues, and made the Party listen so that they could think about how they could help.

In the 1980s and later I invited members of the Young Conservatives to my home. They visited several times over the years and it was helpful as they came willingly, and we discussed what they were working on, and also talked about some of the Conservative MPs and candidates.

I also created the Concourse Group, which was aimed at involving the missing generation of young business and professional people under the age of forty-five. This was all part of my bid to bring the Party up to date, and use its members more efficiently.

The National Union Executive Committee

In 1975 I became a member of the Executive Committee of the National Union, which ran the voluntary side of the Party.

After a while I stood for election for Chairmanship of the main Committee, and again ran into a degree of anti-Semitism. However, I had support and got in, with the help and encouragement of Margaret Thatcher, Lord Carrington and many others – which meant that the Old Guard had to wake up and see that the world had changed!

In 1978 I became Chairman of Greater London Area, and received a letter from Lord Thorneycroft – then Party Chairman – which read:

I would like to put on record my congratulations upon your appointment as Chairman for the Greater London Area. I know your previous years' efforts within that Area have been much appreciated by all – both within the Area, and within the National Union. The times ahead are certainly challenging ones, and I know that Greater

London – capably led here at Central Office by Donald Stringer – will produce magnificent results when the General Election is finally upon us.

In the *Evening News* of 16 March there is a photograph of me in *Money News*, and a paragraph by City Editor Derek Porter saying, 'Basil, who has chided me for suggesting that the Tory Party should try harder to put over its economic policy in the City, says he will be adopting a more positive approach on economic matters in his speechmaking.

'Good for you Basil!'

From Tony Kerpel – President of the Democrat Youth Community of Europe – I received a letter which I called 'magnificent' in my reply to him. He told me:

I was delighted to hear the good news. So often in this funny Party one gets depressed about the sort of people who are popularly selected by the activists, and then along comes a decision based on merit – which restores one's faith. Your win is just such a morale-boosting achievement. We both have a certain amount in common – relative latecomers to the Party, and with little patience for the time-servers and Buggins-turn types. We speak our minds, and that always entails risks. But we both seem to have been accepted because of an ability to deliver the goods, and that application of merit as an arbiter of leadership positions is a great encouragement.

CHAPTER FOURTEEN

PRE-ELECTION RALLIES

In 1983 – just before the General Election – I organised a Conservative Youth Rally at Wembley. There were – of course – the usual detractors, but it was a great success; it was huge, and full of razzamatazz.

We got the young people involved, and the event was jointly compèred by Bob Monkhouse and Jimmy Tarbuck. I had first met Bob and Jimmy while on holiday in Barbados, and when I needed to ask someone to do the honours it was easy for me to decide whom to approach – and I had a pretty good idea that they would accept. They made themselves available to help whenever possible, and also put us in touch with many other celebrities who were sympathetic to the Party cause.

Bob was a talented, seemingly effortless, comedian. His method of compèring the rallies was completely off the cuff – although he knew who everyone was, and was able to say something relevant about each of them. Jimmy Tarbuck also did his homework beforehand, so that he would be well prepared.

At the 1983 rally they introduced an impressive array of stars, including – amongst others – Bryan Forbes and Nanette Newman, Steve Davis, Freddie Trueman, Sharron Davies, Suzanne Dando,

Janet Brown and Michael Winner. Lynsey de Paul composed a special song for the occasion:

> Vote Tory, Tory, Tory
> For Election glory
> We don't want U-turns
> So we'll vote for Maggie T
> Vote Tory, Tory, Tory
> The only Party for me
> Say 'No' to Labour
> And 'No' to SDP.

One person hit the headlines and newspaper cartoons in no uncertain terms. Tiny ball of uncontrollable fire, Kenny Everett, addressed the crowds in his inimitable way:

'Let's bomb Russia!' he cried, and then, 'Let's kick Michael Foot's sticks away!'

Even he, however, thought that he might have been pushing it. Afterwards he cried on Gita's shoulders, saying, 'Oh dear, I think I might have gone a bit too far!'

After all this, Maggie appeared on stage accompanied – as always – by Denis who sported a large cartoon hand, which stated *'Vote For Maggie'*.

In contrast to all the tomfoolery she was very prim and proper – but it made no difference to the crowd as everyone screamed for her. They always did!

We held another pre-Election Rally in 1987 (billed as a 'Family Rally') and another in 1992 which featured Tim Rice, Henry

Cooper, Leslie Crowther, Jim Davidson, Jimmy Greaves and – of course – the Prime Minister, John Major.

We became good friends with all the celebrities – and particularly with Bob Monkhouse whom we used to meet each Christmas on our annual holidays to Barbados. He was a great supporter – both of the Party and of our rallies – and was absolutely brilliant, full of wit and humour. Wherever he was in the world he would send me jokes to use in my speeches – pages and pages of them, although most were so blue I couldn't possibly use them!

Gita recalls:

'Bob gave the most marvellous parties. Everyone there was a comedian. They were always such funny evenings that my stomach hurt from laughing at the end of the evening!'

I was asked to contribute to a book about him called *Bob Monk-house Unpublished!*, written by David Ismay and Chris Gidney (JR Books, 2010) and, of course, I was more than happy to do so.

My excerpt read as follows:

I've been a fan and admirer of Bob's as far back as I can remember. It was a piece of good luck when Gita and I bumped into him many years ago – when he and Jackie were checking into Sandy Lane in Barbados, just as we were getting ready to return to the UK at the end of our holiday. From that moment onwards we saw and spoke to each other regularly.

In those days I was travelling all around the country, in my role as Chairman of the Conservative Party National Union Executive Committee, and I needed some good lines and jokes – which Bob was always willing to provide.

I organised large rallies at Wembley prior to several of the General Elections, when Mrs Thatcher (as she was then) came to 'rally the troops'. Bob helped bring together a group of well-known personalities who would be willing to appear on stage at each event. There was no fuss, no saying 'I'm too busy' – he just said 'yes' to all my requests, offering to compère the shows, and made them days to remember.

And always his jokes kept arriving in the post...

Bob died on 29 December 2003, to our great sadness.

He was a very loyal friend – well loved by us both, as well as by other people from all walks of life. He was highly intelligent, spontaneously brilliant, and always amusing.

Although his humour could be quite blue at times, he still remained the perfect gentleman – very attentive and an excellent listener.

We still miss him.

CHAPTER FIFTEEN

THE CONSERVATIVE PARTY I KNEW

I was – and remain – a great fan of Margaret Thatcher, and owe her a great deal.

She understood the Old Guard's resistance to change – having had her share of criticism and nasty comments from within the Party when she started. I think we recognised the same energy and dynamism in each other, and therefore there was never any dillydallying – once she was convinced of an idea, it was all systems go.

When she came into power she asked me to become part of her inner circle, but for some reason I felt that this was not appropriate at the time, probably because I felt it might conflict with the work I was doing within the National Union. I have always rather regretted this.

David McDonough recalls:

When she said, 'Basil is my kind of man,' other people fell in behind her. He had put some noses out of joint and, frankly, most jolly well deserved it. In the past forty years few people have consistently done as much for the Party as he has.

With Baroness Thatcher, 1985 Party Conference

Margaret Thatcher was all that people say she was – and more. Intelligent, determined and intent on bringing the Conservative Party into the modern twentieth century. She understood the aspirations of the British people, enjoyed great support within the grass roots of the Party and her great skill was in encouraging them to support her, and believe in themselves.

She was also beautiful and had a warm heart, which is something that was rarely publicised.

Gita recalls:

Denis was a real character. He was very smart and rather dashing, often wearing a big black cape when it was cold. He had a good sense of humour and could be very acerbic. Nevertheless, his role in Maggie's life was a vital one – he supported her in everything she did.

I sat next to him at dinner once, and he said that he was the appendage – the man in the joke, who always sits behind the Lady Mayoress. 'Come on,' I told him, 'you know it's Pygmalion. You are the man behind the girl!' He really loved and supported her.

With Denis and Baroness Thatcher, 1985 Party Conference

Margaret invited us to Chequers fairly often when I was running the voluntary party, which was always an enormous thrill. Carol Thatcher describes it in an article she wrote for the *Mail*, 'Ahead of us, down the gun-barrel-straight Victory Drive, lined with magnificent beech trees given by Churchill, was a gracious, discreet rose-red brick and grey stone Tudor building.'

Her mother took us round it, and past the swimming pool which she never used, saying, 'We can't afford to run it!' – the US Ambassador had it installed as a gift when he visited some years before, and found that there was not one there.

Carol, in the same article, remembers:

Sipping coffee (with Lord Thorneycroft) at one end of the orangery that housed a delectable indoor swimming pool.

Knowing my mother wouldn't take a dip because of the threat to her hairdo, I had looked forward to doing many lengths in a virtually private pool. No such luck. Mum discovered it would cost £15,000 a year to heat, so the boiler was turned off! Even the pool didn't escape a wave of her thrifty wand.

On our tour, Mrs Thatcher pointed to the stained glass windows which bore the coats of arms of previous Prime Ministers. There was one notable omission: 'We are still waiting for Ted Heath's,' she said wryly.

Gita recalls:

Before dinner one evening we had drinks in one of the drawing rooms. In this room was a table which had belonged to Napoleon and on the table there stood a small box with a beautiful ring inside it. It had belonged to Anne Boleyn and had also been worn by Elizabeth I for all of her life. It was quite lovely – gold, with ivory and enamel on the inside, and I asked if I could try it on. 'Of course,' said Mrs Thatcher, understanding another woman's interest. I did so, and when we were called down to dinner took it back off and left it on the table where it had been.

The next time we went, when John Major was PM, the ring had been locked away in a strong plastic case with an alarm attached to the outside of it. It will certainly never be left on a table in full view again, so I am therefore probably the last person ever to put it on my finger!

During John Major's term as Prime Minister, Gita and I once again visited Chequers. Initially we went alone, but then I suggested that it would be a great thrill for the twelve Conservative Area Chairman to be invited, and he agreed. They came and had a good time, and went away feeling appreciated. That was valuable, and I wasn't shy about asking.

John Major and I have a close – and frank – relationship, to use a well-worn phrase. I also helped to raise money for the charity his wife Norma supported – Mencap.

We have also visited Willie Whitelaw at Dorneywood, the Chancellor's official residence. It is a Queen Anne-style house, built in the eighteenth century, and owned by the National Trust. The gardens can be visited during the season, but not, of course, the house, which is the country home of a senior member of the Government.

Gita remembers:

The conversation was not always about lofty affairs of state. I can remember, one evening before dinner listening to a couple of guests discussing the merits of the Hokey carpet sweeper! And in one room we found Ken Baker, then Minister of Education, busy doing a jigsaw.

The country was in a bad way when Willie invited us one evening, to dine with, amongst others, Jimmy Tarbuck and Bob Monkhouse.

He came up to me afterwards and said, 'Basil, I don't know what to do about the country – what do you think?'

Gita was delighted – 'Good heavens, Basil, you are running the country now, giving the Deputy Prime Minister advice,' she said with a big smile.

Willie's wife Celia used to go to Joe Corvo, a zone therapist, whom I had also visited every Friday morning for many years. He had several celebrity and royal clients; he looked after Prince Philip's bad arthritis, and Sarah Ferguson went to him too.

Rather predictably, Willie thought it a load of rubbish. He was patrician and rather no-nonsense, and that sort of thing was not at all up his street. He was never a close friend – and, indeed, was not easy to get close to – so people either loved him or were non-committal.

I got to know him better at Party Conferences, and liked him, realising that he appreciated it if you spoke honestly and openly to him. He was also very supportive once he was on your side, as Margaret recognised, when she said, 'Everyone needs a Willie in their lives.'

There are, of course, others who have made a particular impression on me during my political life, including John Bercow, the diminutive Speaker of the House of Commons, who was a strong and effective Head of the Young Conservatives, and an excellent right-wing speaker.

One other person whom I have always admired is Nigel Lawson. He is a very clever man whose actions helped get Britain out of a mess very like the one we are in now, but much more quickly.

Whenever I have approached Nigel over the years, to ask if he would be willing to let me use the facilities of No. 11 for one of my events – be it a reception for the Conservative National Golf Tournament, the London Arts Season, or whatever – he has always been happy to oblige. We still have lunch together from time to time – and on the last occasion, when I asked him if he would be willing to speak at a Renaissance Forum Dinner, he replied, 'I tend not to accept invitations to speaking engagements these days, Basil – but since it's you...'

When I was Chairman of the National Union, I also chaired the Selection Group that interviewed potential parliamentary candidates. One day someone looking rather like a large and rumpled St Bernard loped into the room, immediately putting up the backs of nearly everyone on the Committee. It was Boris Johnson who was then a journalist in Europe, and he thought he would like to be an MP.

Boris was funny, but didn't always seem to take matters seriously, and when he left, everyone said they didn't want him. It was therefore up to me to decide; I felt that he was obviously intelligent and could do a great deal for the Party, but right now he needed a kick in the pants to get him to understand what was needed.

I thought he deserved one more chance, and so I schmoozed and cajoled the others to allow me to do so.

I called Boris later, told him that he had made an appalling first impression and that if he wanted to become an MP he would need the support of the Committee. 'I know you have the ability,' I told him, 'but they want to get rid of you. Come to the next Selection Committee – and this time, behave sensibly!' He did, and the rest is history.

Boris is very clever, and really cares about doing a good job. However, he is not tolerant of what he considers other people's idiocy; he says what he thinks, and this doesn't always make him friends.

Before he stood for Mayor of London against Ken Livingstone I ran an event to bring together a number of important and influential people and convince them to vote for the then-Conservative candidate Steve Norris. However, his candidacy – as we now know – was not successful.

I have not used a car for years, preferring to take cabs whenever I need to get anywhere. I have therefore chatted to many drivers who work in London day in day out, and was able to ask them what they thought. I brought together a group of cab owners, and discussed the situation with them. They were all of the opinion that Livingstone was not on their side, and went out to their drivers to warn them.

The drivers were cautious, however, feeling that they couldn't support anyone else because if they did they would be penalised if Livingstone were to be voted back in. Therefore, when Boris became the new Mayor, most taxi drivers heaved a huge sigh of relief.

William Hague is another person whom I have always admired. He was a very young Leader of the Party, and he is a very good politician. His maiden Conference speech at the age of sixteen caused a sensation, showing us all this chap from the north of England with a round face and a wide smile was certainly someone to watch!

William went into politics in 1983, but became Leader at a difficult time and at the end of his term I think he felt that enough was enough and decided to move to the back benches. He has certainly grown in stature over the years and has always had a reputation as brilliant speaker. At the time of writing he is an excellent Minister of Foreign Affairs – a steady and knowledgeable hand on the international tiller.

When he resigned as Party Leader in 2001, I wrote him a letter expressing my regret, and received a warm one in return, thanking me for my good wishes:

> We threw everything into the Election campaign, and fought a good fight, but in current circumstances we could not prevail. I believe strongly and passionately in everything I have fought for, but it is also vital for leaders to listen and parties to change. In light of the result I thought it right to resign as Leader, but I shall continue to give my full support to my colleagues, and to the Conservative Party.
>
> The forces of Conservatism will continue to strengthen and I have no doubt that we will return to Government in the future. I consider my four years as Leader to have been a great privilege and I have enjoyed every single day. My only regret is that I was unable to lead Conservative candidates, members, voters and the people who supported me as splendidly as you, to the victory they deserved.
>
> Ffion joins me in sending you and Gita our best wishes and our heartfelt thanks for your support, guidance and never-ending kindness.

David Cameron is another impressive person, albeit in a different way. He takes politics very seriously indeed, and his charisma and intelligence were obvious from the first time I met him.

I can recall him coming along to a meeting of one of the

committees I was chairing. David walked in, listened for a while, and then soon took over the proceedings. That was many years ago, and I was therefore not the least surprised when he was made PM in 2005.

David is a good and caring man, and a good Prime Minister, with the interests of the country at heart, and the brains to make sure it is run well. Since forming a coalition with the Liberals at the last Election he has had to work hard to ensure that all sides are happy with the compromises that have needed to be made, but he has done this with great skill. He also continues to do everything he can to ensure we maintain our presence on the world stage.

Ever since he became PM I have known that I could approach him for support and help with any of my projects, and although – these days – I have taken something of a back seat from day-to-day politics, we still remain in touch with each other.

CHAPTER SIXTEEN

THE BRIGHTON BOMB, 1984

The Grand Hotel is an elegant white stucco building on the Brighton seafront, more than a century old. A weekend in Brighton is often code for a bit of hanky panky (of which the Grand may – or may not – have its fair share) but it keeps its cool. Its pillars, gold leaf and sweeping staircase remain gracious and unspoiled.

It was therefore the perfect place for Margaret Thatcher's Cabinet and colleagues to stay during the October 1984 Conservative Party Conference – solid, smart, comfortable Victorian grandeur, with enough space, good food and all mod cons.

Gita and I had a lovely room on the third floor, with a bay window overlooking the sea. Along the corridor, at the corner of the building, Alistair McAlpine, the Party Treasurer, had his room, and we had been invited to go along on that first night for drinks with him and other close colleagues.

Alistair was in good spirits – as we all were. I asked him why he had chosen to stay in such a small room, situated at the corner of the hotel, rather than take his usual – and more spacious – accommodation.

'I bet there will be a fire,' he laughed. 'The fire escape is through my bathroom, and with my luck I'll be starkers in the bath when the alarm goes off, and then find I'm sitting here trying to hide my big tummy, as people troop past me!'

On our arrival we spoke to several friends and as we circulated the room we noticed that, amid all of the hubbub, Norman and Margaret Tebbit were watching a television news report of a train crash – both greatly concerned, and wondering aloud what could be done. This was so typical of them; Norman, then President of the Board of Trade, is a strong man, and his no-nonsense reputation is well deserved. However, he and his wife have warm and generous hearts, and he genuinely cares about other people. Before entering into politics he had been a pilot in the RAF; he is a patriot and a very good friend.

The evening continued – with a mix of business and pleasure – as we all prepared for the next day, when the Conference would open at the Brighton Dome, that enormous Regency edifice attached to Nash's Pavilion, where the Prince Regent's horses were stabled in the eighteenth century.

Gita and I went to several parties before dinner, meeting Sir Anthony Berry on the way to one of them. We had a chat, as we always did, and then went our separate ways – he to a reception, and we back to our room, where we slept, lulled by the sound of the waves.

Then, in the middle of the night, we were woken by a most enormous bang. I rolled over and tried to go back to sleep, because it takes more than a huge noise to disturb my slumbers! However, Gita shook me awake, saying she thought someone was shooting at the hotel from the sea. I looked at my clock on the bedside table, and saw that it was 2.54 a.m.

Dressing as quickly as I could, I ventured outside to see what was happening, and to find out if there was anything I could do to help.

Gita followed, still in her nightie, and we were greeted by people milling around – all wondering what on earth had happened.

We ran back into the room, and in no time at all Gita had managed to get dressed and grasp her small travelling bag which she always takes with her, which contains a change of clothes, her make-up and that sort of thing 'just in case'. Later that evening a lot of people had cause to be very grateful for her presence of mind!

Never an early riser, I was less efficient; in my hurry to leave the room, I left my expensive watch on the bedside table. My faith in human nature was restored, however, when it was returned to me some two weeks later.

We hurried along to Alistair McAlpine's room and clambered one after the other down the steep fire escape ladder (luckily he was not in the bath at the time!) I remember helping one elderly lady down the stairs, and it was with great relief that we all made it to the pavement outside.

Of course at that time we had no idea what had actually happened, and people were running about and shouting for help, followed closely by a posse of men in uniform (police, paramedics etc.) and one man wearing a hard hat who told us in no uncertain terms to 'Stay out!'

We were all ushered onto the beach, where we watched people coming out of the hotel covered in fine white dust. It was a beautiful night and initially the atmosphere amongst us was rather lighthearted, because at that time we had no idea that we had escaped – quite literally – from a bomb site.

Despite the lateness of the hour Margaret Thatcher emerged fully dressed. She had been in her room on the first floor, making the final amendments to her speech for the next day, and hadn't yet gone to bed.

Some while later we were all despatched to different hotels, which took us in and gave us hot drinks and other refreshment. At this stage we still didn't realise the enormity of the situation and fully expected to be allowed back into our rooms at some point the next day.

It was only when we read the next day's newspapers that we learnt with horror that five people had been killed by the bomb, including our good friend, Conservative MP and Treasurer of the Household, the Hon. Sir Anthony Berry, whose room in the hotel had been just two away from ours.

He had just returned from taking his small dog for a walk and when the bomb went off he fell three storeys to the ground floor. Sir Anthony's wife was also injured in the blast, although she later recovered from her injuries. The dog – amazingly – was fine.

Parliamentary Treasury Secretary Sir John Wakeham's wife Roberta was killed, and both Sir Donald Maclean and his wife, Muriel (who were in the room in which the bomb had been placed), were badly injured. Lady Maclean later died.

The other casualties were Eric Taylor, the North West Area Chairman, and Jeanne Shattock, wife of Sir Gordon Shattock, the Western Area Chairman of the Party. Sir Gordon escaped death, but was permanently deafened by the blast.

The explosion took out the whole of the central part of the hotel, which crashed eight floors down to the basement. Amongst those trapped in the rubble were Sir Norman Tebbit and his wife, Margaret, and it took several hours for firemen to rescue them.

I can remember the look of agony on Norman's face as he was finally stretchered out of the hotel. He had a huge gash on his hip, and sustained other injuries from which he has – as much as is possible – recovered. Sadly Margaret sustained more serious injury, and has been left permanently disabled.

In all, thirty-four people were later taken to the Royal National Orthopaedic Hospital in Hertfordshire to be treated, and to recover from their injuries. I visited both Norman and Margaret Tebbit on several occasions while they were at the RNOH, and it was because of this initial contact with the hospital that I later went on to try and help them with their rebuilding plans.

The bomb – a 100-pounder – had been planted several weeks before the Conference by Patrick Magee of the IRA – and they later issued a statement saying, 'Today we were unlucky – but remember, we only have to be lucky once; you will have to be lucky always. Give Ireland peace, and there will be no war.'

The IRA was unlucky in one respect: Margaret and Denis Thatcher escaped unscathed, and Margaret's popularity soared. Her coolness, both during and after the event, was greatly admired – and true to form, instead of sending us home as we all expected, she told us that everything would carry on as scheduled.

The Conference opened as planned at 9.30 a.m., and Margaret appeared on the platform to tumultuous applause, with all her ministers standing up there beside her. I remember Gita noting with rather wry amusement that everyone on the front row still had the price tags showing on the soles of their shoes! Marks & Spencer had opened up especially early to allow everyone to kit themselves out in respectable clothes, sending the bills on later.

The explosion was a vicious and terrifying event, nothing less than a cold-blooded attempt to murder the Cabinet. It could have been far worse than it was, had the Victorians not been such solid and skilful builders, according to the firemen who were interviewed afterwards. However, this was not much consolation to John Wakeham, Donald Maclean, and all the other victims of the bomb and their families.

After hours of worry our son Steven managed to get a call through to us to check we were alive and well. We were able to reassure him we had survived completely unscathed, although the memory of people scuttling about in a frenzy of fear and incomprehension is something that will never leave us.

On the first Saturday after the attack, Margaret Thatcher spoke quite brilliantly to her constituents, saying,

> We suffered a tragedy not one of us could have thought would happen in our country. However we picked ourselves up and sorted ourselves out, as all good British people do – and I thought 'let us stand together, for we are British!'
>
> They were trying to destroy the fundamental freedom that is the birthright of every British citizen – Freedom, Justice and Democracy.

In my role as Chairman of the National Union I chaired the Party Conference in 1985, one year after the bomb, and can recall the tumultuous applause Lord Tebbit received when he appeared on the stage on his return to front-line politics.

With Baroness Thatcher and Lord Tebbit at the 1985 Party Conference, one year after

the bomb

CHAPTER SEVENTEEN

BRINGING FUNDRAISING
UP TO DATE

I was much exercised about the application of the American approach to fundraising.

I had, in the past, arranged (and paid) for some of the leading Republican professionals to come over to England and speak to our professionals and leading members of the National Union. I was still keen to do this – either in England or the States.

I wrote a paper – which was essentially notes to discuss with Lord Thorneycroft – about the application of this American approach to fundraising, and needed to discuss all manner of issues.

Fundraising, I thought, should use direct mail, the telephone and general leadership. On the computer there should be membership information (remember, this was in the early 1970s), voter information, and vote analysis – and I wanted to promote the use of the phone for fundraising and electioneering, something still not completely accepted by the older Party officials.

I suggested a management workshop, and survey research. Posters, photographs, radio and television were also on my list, to make sure everyone knew who people were, and were thus encouraged to vote for them. Above all, I was very keen for the Party in the UK to meet the Americans, here or there, and see for themselves how effective their methods were.

In the Conservative Party of the 1970s, apart from some forward-looking individuals such as Margaret Thatcher, this was a lot like recommending we canvass in swimsuits, or visit by coming down the chimney. The 'Old Guard' certainly thought it would be just as intrusive. However, I saw my task as proving the worth of the US methods to the dissenters in our Party.

Another of my papers with this aim was 'The Telephone – A Real Political Asset'. I outlined the way the telephone could help us – canvassing, knocking up, survey canvassing, contact with voters in general.

'Let's scotch the familiar indictment: they only come to see us when they want our vote,' I suggested, and followed this up with a training scheme. I felt people should be armed with prepared scripts, and trained how to use them by a coach, using tape recorders to show up and deal with mistakes.

I was firm about calls being at 'sensible and convenient times' and stressed, 'A telephone operation must be seen as a saving. Apart from convenience and speed of communication, telephoning saves petrol, manpower and shoe leather. It also ignores bad weather.'

I suggested political messages be recorded, to be used in three different ways. One was for canvassing, with Mrs Thatcher's voice on tape. Another was her voice again, pointing out the urgent necessity of the household voting. The last one was a system that might be known as 'dial-a-policy'. Central Office would have perhaps six phones installed, each programmed with an answering service, dealing with six different areas of policy. Local organisations would send out, in their election literature, the telephone numbers which interested voters can ring, if they wished to know the outline of specific Conservative policies.

I urged that at all times telephone calls which prove at all fruitful should be followed up immediately by a letter and personal visit, if possible.

However sensible and run of the mill all this seems now, let me assure you that it was not received enthusiastically by everyone in the Party. Much of it was looked upon as more of Feldman's 'smart arsery' and some of the more hidebound members of the Party wished heartily that I would go away and leave them alone – not the people who really mattered, however, who allowed me to go ahead.

The results I achieved spoke for themselves. The American example was informative, inspiring and a little daunting, especially in the face of a distinct lack of overall enthusiasm. But we used a lot of what we learnt.

The *Daily Telegraph* ran an Election Scrapbook by Onlooker, and mentioned 'Dial-a-Maggie':

> During the closing days of the campaign, voters will be able to hear the latest message from Margaret Thatcher by telephone, as they dial for the weather forecast or the latest test score.
>
> The Tories are believed to be the first political party to use the telephone in this way for electoral purposes.

This was my idea. It took a lot of pushing, and solid determination, but I knew it would work – and it did!

Patrons' Club

In August 1990 I commissioned Tim Haines (Prize Research Fellow in American Studies at Nuffield College, Oxford) and Edmund Lazarus to produce 'A Business Plan for a National Patrons' Club for the Conservative Party', along the lines of the very productive Republican Clubs in the United States.

Tim went to the USA for a month to research the paper, visiting Washington, Florida and San Francisco.

The aim of the Patrons' Club, according to their paper, was to 'Raise £5,000,000 per annum from up to 1,000 donors – each contributing a minimum of £5,000 per year by means of a club'.

The short document also covered initial requirements, recruitment and events, and moved on to medium- and long-term organisation and costs.

Twelve people plus an Executive President were needed – drawn from different regions, backgrounds and communities. Their membership subscriptions (£85,000 altogether) would cover the initial costs, and thus avoid any financial input from Central Office.

Sir Philip Harris (now Lord Harris of Peckham), Lord Beaverbrook and the authors of the report would assemble this group, and they asked me to be Chairman – with Beaverbrook as my deputy. Each of us would recruit twenty people, who would also – later – be asked to recruit more members, taking the total membership up to the required 1,000. Frances Prenn was appointed Executive Director, and was responsible for organisation and management from Central Office.

The first year revenue targets were more modest – in the region of £65,000 by late October 1990 – but they were planned to increase as the membership multiplied.

In October that year we met with Tim Bell – the Conservative Party advertising guru – and followed it up with a letter covering the things we had discussed. It was mostly about the name for the new club, and several suggestions were made – including Common Ground, which I liked a lot. Nevertheless I asked for his input.

I told him that the club should stand for Conservatives who were interested in the success of Government and who would like to use the club to meet like-minded Conservatives and to help with the Party. We would offer them – in exchange for their membership fee of either £500 or £1,000 a year – two issues of newsletter, a reception or dinner for which they could buy tickets, some form of regular phone contact to get their views (possibly the most valuable benefit of all) – and not forgetting the sartorial element, we offered a club tie and badge for men and a scarf and badge for women. The point was to create long-term relationships which, we hoped, would result in increased giving.

The club was run from Central Office and its financial management was completely transparent. All income was handed to the Conservative Board of Finance (CBF) and it maintained a record of income and expenses. Every December there was an annual budget review, when a budget had to be approved by Party Treasurers. Any such approved expense would then be sanctioned by the Executive Director and paid for by the CBF. Any extra expenses had to be approved by a Party Treasurer before they were incurred.

Learning from the American approach

In 2001, at my instigation, Michael Spencer, Olivia Bloomfield and Diana Berry went to Washington to update themselves on the states of US political fundraising and to bring what they found out back to the Party.

Their three-day visit was an eye-opener. An average donation was $65 from each of the 1.3 million donors. Telefundraising was focused on by the National Republican Senatorial Committee (NRSC); they ran a call centre, which always used a home number, and always called with an issue – the donors apparently enjoyed a good fight, and phoners could respond to the challenge if they so wished. Donors could opt out of being called but otherwise they could expect to be phoned every ninety days. Only 25 per cent of people hung up immediately.

One particularly successful campaign involved sending a dollar bill to prospective members – it got an excellent 18 per cent response. Seventy per cent of funds were raised from telemarketing and 30 per cent from donations.

Some of the numbers involved were eye-watering! The annual NRSC Presidential Gala for 5,500 guests raised $32 million.

Everyone was photographed with the President (this was called a 'goat rope'). Exclusive events at a private house with no press were successful, relaxed lobster nights or cocktail parties for a minimum of 175 guests were fruitful, as was a celebrity fight between Mayorga and De La Hoya, organised by Don King for donor club members at $1,200 per ticket.

Donor clubs were also long-established and extremely profitable. The Republican Regents had 400 members who paid $50,000 in a two-year cycle, with spouses being able to join at $25,000. The Republican Eagles was the oldest club – formed in 1975 – with members who gave $15,000 a year to the candidates, who would do one event a week at least.

It was considered Bush's master stroke that he introduced graded fundraising; Pioneers paid $10,000, Rangers $200,000 and Mavericks (aged twenty-five to forty) having to raise $50,000. The Majority makers raised $25,000 a year – members being allowed to attend the President's Dinner.

Janice Knopp, the Finance Director of the National Republican Congressional Committee concerned with increasing Republican seats in the House of Representatives, made full use of politicians in person to fundraise. 'A typical Congressman,' she said, 'could hope to raise between $1.5 million and $4.5 million in pledges, according to where they were.' She recommended broadening the donor base when the going was good, to insure against the inevitable lean times.

There were other powerful tools that I wanted to introduce to the Conservative Party:

- Single-message causes were powerful, especially with young professionals
- People's contributions at dinners increased the nearer they sat to the candidate
- If you booked a table, or brought a party, you got a better deal
- It was very important to get a list of people for the candidate to approach

Fran Katz, Bill Clinton's fundraiser, recommended:

- Have a good list
- Know how to build it

- Know how to manage it
- Maintain your relationships
- The candidate should make their own calls for about two hours, three days a week

Never a dull moment!

It was exhausting for everyone, but the atmosphere crackled and America certainly knew who was who and what their vote (and their donation) got them.

I was convinced that we, in the UK, could take plenty from their approach and make a real difference to the Party.

UK Donor Clubs

As a result of studying this American approach, I was inspired to start and run Team 1,000, then the Front Bench Club, and ultimately the Renaissance Forum (which I chaired from 1998 to 2010). Membership of these clubs depended on the level of membership paid.

Other groups – run by other people – were the Shadow Chancellor's Group and the Leader's Group.

My idea for the Renaissance Forum was to hold regular dinners with a variety of guest speakers. I chose not to restrict these speakers to politicians – instead, over the years, inviting everyone from Ambassadors to journalists, opinion formers and commentators – everyone, in fact, who I felt had something positive to offer, and a professional knowledge of the subject being discussed.

Attendance at dinners was normally restricted to thirty, with many more being invited to the annual 'member and partner' dinner.

People got to know each other, and it made a lot of friends for the Party.

Our first dinner – with my brother-in-law, William Safire, as guest speaker – took place on 20 April 1998. Since then we have held dinners covering a variety of different topics, with speakers such as:

- Sir Clive Thompson of Rentokil and the Italian Ambassador, who discussed the merits (or otherwise) of the Single Currency
- Charles Moore (the former *Daily Telegraph* editor), Lord Saatchi and Nicholas Sparrow of ICM to discuss ways of winning the General Election
- Greg Dyke, when he was Director General of the BBC
- George Osborne MP
- William Hague MP
- David Davis MP
- Liam Fox MP
- Lord King of Bridgwater
- Michael Portillo MP
- Andrew Neil
- Stephen Gilbert
- Andy Coulson
- Lord Tebbit
- Trevor Philips OBE
- David Starkey (historian)
- Peter Oborne (former political editor of *The Spectator*)

And many, many others.

We normally served the meal first, and then our guest speaker addressed us for about fifteen minutes or so, before we moved on to questions. However, on one occasion I remember we had invited the Chinese Ambassador to be our guest of honour, and he said he would prefer to speak before we started our meal. He spoke fluently for about fifty minutes, and it was impossible to stop him, although by that time we were all getting rather hungry. He was very interesting, but our attention was beginning to wander and so I had to step into the breach and bring his observations to a close – much to the relief of the assembled company. If I had not, I fear that we would possibly still be there – with the delicious aroma of dinner wafting past our nostrils.

We always held an annual black tie member and partner dinner – and often these dinners took place in the glorious surroundings of Thomas Goode, which for one night was transformed into a glamorous dining room.

Renaissance Forum Dinner at Thomas Goode (l–r: Michael Spencer, William Hague, Lord Feldman, Ffion Hague, Rumi Verjee [owner of Thomas Goode])

In 2009 David Cameron was our guest of honour at the annual dinner (the Leader of the Party normally attends these dinners). Our dinner took place just prior to the General Election and I can recall Boris Johnson – then newly elected Mayor of London – popping in for a drink to show his support and solidarity.

In total Sheila (my PA) and I have organised more than 120 dinners. We have sweated blood and tears over our seating plans; sometimes we have spotted a potential problem, but we have always managed to rearrange the tables in good time.

In 2010 I decided that it was time for me to stand down as Chairman of the Forum, and to hand over the running of the club to a younger man. We therefore chose James Stewart to be its new Chairman, although I remain as Club President.

Unbeknownst to me, the Forum members had told Sheila that they wanted to present me with a gift to mark my years of service. After much deliberation they chose a beautiful silver quaich (Scottish communal drinking bowl) which John Major presented to me on their behalf.

With Sir John Major on my retirement as Renaissance Forum Chairman

He made a wonderful speech – ad-libbing all the way through – and I was delighted to be given such a lovely gift, which – I am happy to say – comes in very handy as a container for my Werther's Originals!

CHAPTER EIGHTEEN

SUNDAY TRADING

D uring my time as Chairman of Better Made in Britain I had got to know many of the leading retail organisations in the country very well. I was therefore pleased to be approached by a consortium of these retailers, to ask if I would be willing to head up a campaign to try and change the Sunday Trading laws ... and I agreed.

The Shopping Hours Reform Council was set up in answer to what, to me and many others, seemed a real need and demand from the buying public. Today it is entirely normal for shops to open on Sundays. The opening hours are shorter (although this is now the subject of debate once more) but otherwise Sunday is pretty much the same as any other day on the retail front. Before 1994, however, things were very different. Shops – like many still today on mainland Europe – remained firmly closed. Some people wanted them to stay that way.

Keep Sunday Special (KSS) was an organisation set up in 1985 by Michael Schluter CBE to campaign energetically against the plans to change the law so that large stores (i.e. those with a retail area of 3,000 square feet or more) could be allowed to extend their opening hours. They wanted only small food and

convenience stores to be allowed to trade, and only garden centres, DIY stores and motor supply shops of over 3,000 square feet
to be open. It believed that opening any other shops on Sundays would have a bad effect on families, communities and local
economies.

Keep Sunday Special had presented their case against any attempt to change the law on Sunday Trading to Alistair Darling,
who had confirmed that the Labour Government was minded to
leave things as they were.

*With David Ramsden and Roger Boaden discussing our plans for Sunday Trading
with members of the public*

The Sunday Trading Campaign – of which I became Chairman –
was launched at the QEII Conference Centre in the late summer of
1988 with the aim of lobbying the Government to change its mind.

We took stands at the various Party Conferences in the autumn of that year with the aim of explaining our stance to as many people as we possibly could.

Working with Phillip Whitehead, Chairman of the Consumers' Association, we had done our homework. A MORI poll we commissioned showed that 67 per cent of those questioned supported our changes to the law (which, Baroness Jay said, was an ass because some 28 million shoppers broke this law every week).

We produced information to put our case. 'Making Sense of Sunday – A Consensus for Reform' was the heading on one brochure we produced. This explained the situation as it was when we started our campaign and outlined a four-point plan to 'resolve the anomalies and put the law in touch with the realities of modern life – while acknowledging the importance of Sunday as a special day with its own character'.

The four points were:

1. Sunday opening hours for all shops
2. All-day opening for small and family shops
3. Protection for shop workers, including a Code of Practice giving shop workers the right not to be dismissed or in any way prejudiced if they refused Sunday work
4. Evening opening during the week – a general allowance for opening hours to be extended to 10.00 p.m., with enforceable safeguards for shop staff

It seemed completely logical but change wasn't easy. This was the only issue that Margaret Thatcher failed to get past the House of

Commons (although she succeeded with the arguably more controversial Poll Tax).

The team working with me at the Shopping Hours Reform Council included:

- Roger Boaden (with whom I had worked closely for many years at Conservative Central Office) who became the Campaign Director
- David Ramsden (formerly Head of Public Affairs at Kingfisher) who became our Deputy Director
- Eleanor Laing MP, Andrew Currie and Laura Sandys

Together with Tony Askham – a lawyer whom we engaged – we decided to find out ways of testing the 1950 Shops Act, which prevented Sunday Trading on the basis that it was damaging to workers.

Roger Boaden recalls:

Basil had approached me with a project: the reform of Sunday Trading. After a lot of discussion, I left the Conservative Party's employment (after almost thirty years), and joined him in setting up the Shopping Hours Reform Council.

I worked with Basil every day for the next four years. It was an exciting and occasionally a bumpy ride, and although we made substantial strides in winning the public argument, we didn't succeed, despite lots of lobbying and publicity.

David Ramsden says:

We thought we had done all that was necessary in 1986, but Margaret Thatcher put the Bill before Parliament and lost. The Sunday Trading Bill had been announced in the Queen's Speech in 1985. For some reason Mrs Thatcher was concerned that any stumbling block would be in the Lords, rather than the Commons, but she was proved wrong (the Lords is a far more radical and reforming House than the Commons will ever be). When it reached the Lords the bench of Bishops – as expected – made their objections, but surprisingly these were on human resources, rather than on theological grounds.

When we set up the Shopping Hours Reform Council Basil agreed to be Chairman (a position he held for five years) with Roger Boaden as Director. At that time no one in the Conservative Party was prepared to reintroduce the failed Bill, and so Basil got to work and looked for a compromise.

He hosted dinners at the Carlton Club for people he wanted to persuade – such as heads of the retail industry who were wavering a little. Both he and Roger also attended our weekly management meetings and did their best to encourage the Party to support us.

Eleanor Laing remembers:

As the campaign progressed, there was concern voiced that this was mainly a Conservative-led campaign, as both Basil and Roger had held long-standing positions within the Party.

Basil decided that he would stand down as Chairman (although he would remain President) and we commenced our search for a replacement. We had approached many people, but one person in particular stood out as the best choice. That person was Baroness Jay, and as she was a Labour Peer no one could now accuse us of having any party bias.

This was all well and good, and we were all beavering away. However, our main opposition came from the Jubilee Centre – a charity based in Cambridge – which ran Keep Sunday Special. They ran a strong campaign, initially persuading the Commons to vote against the Bill by getting people to write hundreds of letters to their MPs, all stating that they would never vote for them again if they allowed the Bill to pass. As David Ramsden said: 'If you get 500 letters and have a 1,000 majority, you think carefully about what you want to support.'

Roger Boaden recalls:

Basil and I met Michael Schluter many times. He was very much a fundamentalist, and there was also a suggestion that he was involved with a US right wing church, with Keep Sunday Special receiving some funding from that source. He and Basil were, of course, civil to each other but I don't think Basil liked him.

Eleanor toured the country in an attempt to gain the support of local groups, who then went on to lobby their local MPs to try and gain support for our campaign in that way. She also did lots of interviews with local television and radio to help spread the message.

In March 1986, the Bill had its second Commons reading, and failed again. (Nine MPs actually flew over from wherever they were to cast their vote against it.) Something else that contributed to its failure was the announcement made at the time that US bombers had taken off from British airfields to bomb Libya. The Unions were also at loggerheads with Mrs Thatcher.

Despite our best efforts, by the summer of 1990 our campaign was running out of steam. It was also felt that the campaign was unlikely to achieve success in that Parliament – mainly because of the possibility of a General Election in 1991, and also the fact that if this Election were to take place, MPs would not want to have to discuss any potentially contentious Bills. Although the Election was not held until 1992 we wound down our operation – with Andrew Currie and Roger Boaden remaining to keep things ticking over, and Baroness Jay remaining as Chairman.

Roger Boaden recalls:

With the change of Leadership of the Party, and the winning of the 1992 General Election by John Major, a number of retailers were becoming agitated by the Bill's lack of progress. This was particularly true of Sainsbury's. One of the main arguments was an objection to our campaign having both leading figures – Basil and myself – with Conservative backgrounds. Basil was recognised as the principal figure – the 'top gun', as they said, in the voluntary ranks of the Party. Sainsbury's pressed for a non-Conservative Chairman, so Basil stood down, I was kept on as a Director with a restricted remit, and Baroness Jay became the new Chairman of the campaign.

Meanwhile, all sorts of anomalies were coming up, and the situation was getting ridiculous.

A furniture retailer started selling bags of carrots (which were exempt under the Act) for hundreds of pounds, so that they could give away a 'free' lounge suite with every purchase. Because motoring accessories were also exempt, a DIY firm built a caravan and fitted it out with everything they had in their shops, even guttering, to demonstrate that the Act allowed them to do this.

Apart from the perceived Conservative bias in the early years of our campaign (which we subsequently dealt with by appointing Baroness Jay) the other main concern expressed by the Unions was the fact that their workers would be forced to work on Sundays.

It seems strange, these days, to think that such a thing could be one of the potential stumbling blocks, because weekends (and particularly Sundays) are the days when there are most women at work in supermarkets and retail stores. Many of these women say that they like the idea that they can earn their own money to help support the family, and they also like that on weekends their partners can take their part in looking after the children. Labour, too, were generally supportive of the Bill as it provided opportunities for workers.

We finally thrashed out an agreement with the Union of Shop, Distributive and Allied Workers (USDAW) that no worker would be forced to work on Sundays against their will, and also put in other safeguards to protect these workers' rights.

A compromise was reached – with Sunday opening being

allowed only between the hours of 10 a.m. and 4 p.m., as a sop to the KSS lobby, and shop workers being protected by having contracts which automatically opted them out of working on Sundays. They had to volunteer to opt in, which many did of course, as they were paid premium rates.

On 19 November 1993 the Sunday Trading Bill was published. It contained three options for reform: total deregulation, a joint regulatory scheme based on the proposals of Keep Sunday Special and the Retailers for Shops Act Reform or a compromise scheme of partial deregulation, based on the proposal of our Shopping Hours Reform Council.

Members of Parliament were given a free vote on this Bill. The first vote was in favour of our scheme, with an agreement of 333 votes to 258. The Bill finished its progress in the Commons on 23 February 1994 and was read a second time in the Lords on 8 March. On 29 March the House was given the same free choice as the Commons between the three options for reform and our scheme was agreed to by a vote of 206 Contents to 151 Non-Contents.

On 5 July 1994 the Sunday Trading Act 1994 received Royal assent, and on 26 August the Act came into force.

Keep Sunday Special, however, didn't go completely quiet, and I believe the organisation still exists. Michael Schluter continued for some time to say that yet another new Act was needed 'to guarantee a shared weekly day off for everyone'.

In 1994 David Southwell – the British Retail Consortium's Director of Communications – said to Sarah Ryle of *The Observer*:

Sunday is the second most popular day for shopping. The people who said it would not work look pretty silly now. We are a multi-faith society. Women are a major part of the workforce, and the idea of having to do the shopping midweek now seems an anachronism. Retail has become a leisure activity – it is not just about chore shopping. Everything has changed – that is why it happened when it did, and why it is successful now.

USDAW were not entirely happy about some developments. For example, they say that the 'browsing hour' which many companies have introduced goes against the spirit of the 1994 legislation, as you still need to have staff available for that.

However, these objections have been addressed and are now almost irrelevant. The Bill was brought in as a commonsense response to a changing society and the need of the retail industry at all levels.

In 1993 John Major appointed David Hunt, an old friend of mine, as Secretary of State for Employment. I explained to him that shop worker protection was the major sticking point. Sometime later, David called me, telling me to buy the *Sunday Express* the next day. It carried a lead story explaining the Government's decision to protect Sunday shop workers. This was a defining moment; it broke the log jam, and the rest, as they say, is history.

Eleanor Laing remembers the campaign being

A fun campaign and also very political – not party politics per se, but political in the way in which it changed attitudes towards Sunday Trading.

Thanks to a lot of effort and campaigning from myself, subsequent Presidents and Chairmen, from Roger, from the heads of retail stores and Members of House of Commons and the House of Lords, Sunday trading is now universal and there is no chance that this will change.

Lord and Lady Whitelaw with members of the Shopping Hours Reform Council

CHAPTER NINETEEN

ENTERING THE LORDS

It all began one day in November 1995. I had been knighted in 1982, and now John Major – the outgoing Prime Minister – wished to offer me a Peerage for Services to Industry and to the Conservative Party.

In 1982 I had received a letter from Garter Principal King of Arms at the College of Arms, congratulating me on my knighthood. I was asked to go to the College to sign the Roll of Knights Bachelor, which is maintained by Garter King of Arms. I was told that I was

> entitled, if I had no Armorial Bearings, to apply for a Grant of Arms and Crest by Letters Patent (this being a document in vellum headed with the Royal Arms) under the hands and seals of the Kings of Arms – they acting in such respect pursuant to their Powers received from the Crown.

I had now received a letter from Her Majesty the Queen, explaining that she was minded to offer me a Peerage – and asking me if I was minded to accept.

I, of course, felt that this was a great honour, and a wonderful way of having my efforts on behalf of my country and my Party recognised – with a chance to do more. I had never aspired to such a position, having previously been delighted at receiving a knighthood, but I obviously accepted her offer.

On the day that the letter arrived I opened it in bed, and after reading the contents, turned over to say, 'Good Morning, Lady Feldman,' to Gita. Rather annoyingly she said that while I might have become a Lord, her name hadn't actually changed, because she was already Lady Feldman as a result of my having been knighted some years previously!

We had to keep the honour a big secret until the formal announcement of the Honours List. However, when we were able to talk about it, we went to see Gita's mother in her nursing home. She was, by then, well into her nineties, but this didn't stop her standing up when we walked in, and giving me a rather graceful curtsey! She was a marvellous lady.

To become a Member of the House of Lords I needed two sponsors, and so I approached Margaret Thatcher and Cecil Parkinson – who both agreed at once. They were the people I had worked with most closely over the years – Margaret when she was Prime Minister and Leader of the Party, and Cecil as Party Chairman, when I was Chairman of the National Union.

Cecil – apart from being a good-looking and popular man – was extremely able and decent, and also very supportive to me. I found him open to ideas, and without his help I could not have put as many of my thoughts into practice as I did. We both wanted to bring the Party more up to date, which we did – with Margaret's blessing.

You had to meet certain requirements to be accepted into the House of Lords, although prior to 2001 the Constitution tended to

be more of an unwritten one, rather than the more precise requirements which are laid down by the Appointments Commission these
days. However, the basic expectation was that you would be able to

- show a record of significant achievement
- make an effective and significant contribution to the work of the
  House of Lords, not only in your area of particular interest and
  special expertise, but also in the wide range of other issues coming
  before the House
- show a willingness to commit the time necessary to make an effective contribution to the work of the House of Lords
- demonstrate outstanding personal qualities – in particular, integ-
  rity and independence
- have independence of Party political considerations, no matter
  what your past Party political involvement

Once the candidate – and their sponsors – have examined their past
(and their consciences), the assessment begins. It doesn't happen
overnight, and is by no means a done deal. Nominees' domicile and
nationality are checked, their suitability matched with published
criteria, and discussed by the Commission's Secretariat. Then the
recommendations are further examined by a sub-committee, and an
interview is set up. References are taken beforehand.

The interview addresses the nominee's skills in relation to the
role of a Peer – for example, will they fit in, play an active part,
not bring dishonour to the House – that sort of thing. After the
interviews, information is reviewed by the Commission, which
then draws up its final list of recommendations.

Once I had my sponsors, and the appointment had been confirmed, I made the requisite trip to Ede and Ravenscroft, the company who make and store the Peers' robes. Some people choose to hire their robes to wear on occasions such as the State Opening, while others (myself included) buy their own set. After each use the robes are returned to Ede and Ravenscroft so that they can be kept fresh and in mint condition, until they are needed again.

It was now up to me to choose a coat of arms, and I was guided through the complexities of this process by Thomas Woodcock in his role as Norroy King of Arms at the College of Arms. He was an enormous help, and I have ended up with a coat of arms that suits my character, my family and my beliefs.

My motto '*Melius Quo Citius*' means 'The Sooner the Better' which everyone agrees is particularly appropriate for me!

My coat of arms

I was finally introduced to the House as Baron Feldman of Frognal (including – in my title – a reference to the area in Hampstead in which I live) on 14 February (Valentine's Day) 1996.

On the morning of my introduction I put on my new robes and then went down to Central Lobby to greet the family. There were about twenty of us present on that occasion, including the grandchildren – who greatly amused themselves by hiding in the folds of my robes, and passing around my hat to try on.

With Gita and the grandchildren, in the Lords Robing Room

Fenella was present and, as she looked up at the balcony where everyone would be sitting during the ceremony, she suddenly broke into song ... 'The Man I Love is Up in the Gallery' – much to the delight of the stewards present.

Waiting to enter the Chamber – with Baroness Thatcher and Lord Parkinson

As we waited to be called into the Chamber I have to admit that I was feeling a little trepidatious as I tried to remember all the things I had been told about what would be required of me during the ceremony. The courtiers had been quite specific in their instructions: one step forward, two steps back, bow, accept my introduction to the Chamber, talk if spoken to, bow again etc. etc. However, much to my family's relief (and my own!) I managed to do everything without making any mistakes.

Black Rod opened the heavy doors to the Chamber, and in we filed – Margaret in front of me, and Cecil following behind. Our heavy red robes swished as we proceeded up the aisle of the

Chamber, which was crowded with my fellow Peers and seemed absolutely enormous. I am not easily intimidated, but the solemnity of the occasion, and our soft footfalls as we walked up the centre of the room in silence, all made me feel very much part of the fabric of Britain – Great Britain.

After the investiture, we celebrated with lunch in the Barry Room. Margaret and Cecil joined us for what was a really jolly occasion – made so by everyone's pleasure and also my own relief that I had not fallen flat on my face in front of my fellow Peers!

With Gita, after the ceremony

Fenella continued to thrill the waiters. As Gita said, all the waiting staff in the Lords thought Peers two a penny – but they were thrilled to have an actress in their midst, telling Fenella that they had loved her for years, and how wonderful it was to meet her.

It was a really lovely day, and my only regret was that neither my mother nor my father was there to share it (although my father had been present when I received my knighthood from the Queen at Buckingham Palace). Had my mother been present, I think she would have giggled!

The Lords is a wonderful place – an intimate club; a place where much of the serious business of Parliament goes on; a very grand historical venue, full of ceremony and grandeur – some of which has not changed for centuries.

The Order of Procession for the State Opening of Parliament says it all:

The Queen is met at Sovereign's Entrance by the Earl Marshal and Lord Great Chamberlain (who have ceremonial and royal parliamentary duties). The Royal Standard is flown from the Victoria Tower and gun salutes are fired by the King's Troop in Hyde Park and the Tower of London.

Wearing the Imperial State Crown and the Robe of State, the Queen emerges from the Robing Room before leading the procession through the Royal Gallery and into the House of Lords Chamber. Four Pages of Honour follow immediately behind the Queen; next come the Captains of the Gentlemen-at-Arms, and the Yeomen of the Guard (the Chief and Assistant Government Whips respectively in the House of Lords). They are followed by the Chief of the Defence Staff, the Comptroller of the Lord Chamberlain's Office and the Field-Officer-in-Brigade-Waiting. The

Lieutenant of the Yeomen of the Guard and his opposite number in the Corps of Gentlemen-at-Arms take up the rear of the procession. The Great Sword of State and the Cap of Maintenance – symbols of sovereign power and authority – are carried in front of the Queen.

It's all arcane, and rather marvellous.

I had waited a few months before I made my maiden speech in the Lords – and finally plucked up the courage to speak, in April 1996, on a debate dealing with tourism and its importance to the UK. I was able to call on my experiences while Chairman of the London Arts Season, and to explain the impact that our work in that area had had on tourism in London.

Later, in May 2000, I took part in an important debate which dealt with the clothing industry. My speech focused on the work I had done with Better Made in Britain, and it went down rather well, I like to think.

Some years later I once again took part in a debate on the Economy, Innovation and Enterprise. I haven't spoken that often – but when I have done it is to speak about a topic on which I have a particular interest or involvement.

A wonderful thing about being in the Lords is that you are at the very heart of what is going on. For example, when President Obama came to visit the UK in May 2011 he spoke to the Lords – walking the entire length of a packed Westminster Hall, shaking hands as he went. It was a marvellous occasion, and I was delighted to be present.

CHAPTER TWENTY

LORDS REFORMS

The Blair Government had reconfirmed its intention to work towards legislation to remove hereditary Peers from the House of Lords, which struck me as a terrible idea.

Forget all the history and tradition. That is – and was – important, of course, but there was also the wealth of experience and sheer hard work that Members put in, and also the House's importance to democracy.

I am not an hereditary Peer, so have no particular axe to grind on my own behalf, but felt very strongly that the part these Peers played in the House of Lords was vital to the sensible running of our country.

Before I entered the Lords, I had visited the House – from time to time – in the course of Party business. I admit that my initial impressions were that it didn't seem to be very busy, and that there did seem to be rather a lot of ancient Members, all snoozing the afternoon away on the red benches! However, this soon proved to be a false impression, and when I became a Peer I soon realised that their contribution was – quite simply – invaluable.

In 1998, and as part of their reforms, the Labour Party was determined to get rid of hereditary Peers. I was therefore asked if I would be part of a small team of three, who had the task of be-coming Trustees, and raising enough money to fight a campaign to prevent this.

Before the 1999 reform there were 1,326 Members of the Lords, of whom 759 were hereditary Peers. Labour's new plan was to have a House dominated by approximately 540 life Peers, including the ninety-seven Labour Peers created since Tony Blair had become Labour Party Leader.

In his time in office, Blair had created more Peers in a shorter space of time than any of his predecessors. In all, he created 386 Peers, in contrast to Harold Wilson's 226 in eight years, Edward Heath's forty-eight in four years, Margaret Thatcher's 216 in eleven years, and John Major's 171 in seven years.

That was what Andrew Marr called 'a Chamber of chums' – and, worse, chums who rarely attended, spoke or voted.

On 30 June 1998 I added my name to those of Lord Denham and Baroness O'Cathain, and sent a letter out to every Member of the House of Lords, explaining our plans to fight to save these hereditary Peers.

The text of our letter was as follows:

The general public has little knowledge of the role of the House of Lords – how it works, how important it is to democracy, and how little it costs. We therefore intend to use the coming months to show the real value and purpose of an effective and independent Second Chamber, and must ensure that reform is introduced in a coherent and responsible way and only after comprehensive discussion.

We sent a form with the letter, asking for contributions to our fund, in order to cover our work, and to hire what we accurately described as 'a small, full-time, dedicated team in order that we can project a properly articulated case, up and down the country'.

This turned out to be extremely successful, with 60 per cent of Conservative Peers – plus Peers from other parties – responding. By 31 July we had received 260 cheques, and in total raised £280,000 to fight our cause.

In October I wrote again to the Lords, pointing out two examples of the value of our work which had received widespread and positive publicity – these were (1) the vote on Scottish university fees, and (2) the vote on the age of consent.

We also got going in order to spread the word about what the Labour Party was planning in detail and also to explain what it is that the Lords does – again in some detail.

For example, it revises badly drafted Bills which come from the Commons, and provides an independent alternative voice in Parliament. (Peers are generally more likely to follow their consciences and vote for a good Bill, rather than just follow the party line of their Whip.)

The Lords scrutinises ministers, asks lots of awkward questions, speaks up on all sorts of causes – regardless of popularity – and is the nearest thing to unbiased Government that we have. Nor is it expensive. It costs a fraction of the cost of the Commons and the European Parliaments; its Members do not receive a salary (unlike the Commons) but merely claim their attendance allowance. I know, too, that many Peers – myself included – don't always claim this allowance.

However, the Lords' main power is to stop a Government from keeping itself in office by refusing to call a General Election after a five-year period. It can't, though, veto any law passed by the Commons.

The first Lords newsletter came out in July 1999. It was written by Roger Rosewell (a *Daily Mail* journalist whom I had appointed to work on our campaign), was published by campaigners for an independent Parliament, and cost the taxpayer nothing at all. The tone was tabloid rather than broadsheet, but the facts it contained were absolutely correct, and not – I am sure – something that Mr Blair felt very comfortable with!

On the front page, under the heading 'Nowhere in the World', we asked the readers to consider what was being planned.

'What's It All About, Tony?' asked the second Lords newsletter – published in October 1999. It challenged the Prime Minister's intentions regarding hereditary Peers and pointed out that the Lords had become the most hard-working Chamber in the world.

It also pointed out something that might, otherwise, have been brushed under the carpet: that, in the 1997/8 session, the Lords sat for 228 days – and on more than 100 occasions, these sessions did not finish until after 10 p.m.

During that period, the Lords had to make almost 4,000 amendments to draft laws, and stood out – for example – against the closed list election system used for the European Elections, and also the imposition of a £1,000 yearly additional charge on English and Welsh students attending Scottish universities.

The Lords also voted that any legal challenge to the number of hereditary Peers be referred to the Committee for Privileges – chaired, at the time, by Lord Slynn of Hadley (who was a Law Lord).

One legal challenge concerned the drafting of the Bill, and declared that an existing Writ of Summons (the document by which Members of each House of Parliament are summoned to serve in that Parliament) would cease to be effective in November 1999. Legal opinion argued that the Writ – once given – could not be overwritten, but that it would endure for the lifetime of a Parliament.

That was one spanner in the Labour works!

Another challenge concerned the place of Scottish Peers in the House. The 1707 Treaty of Union determined that there should be sixteen Peers in the House of Lords to represent Scotland, and this could not be set aside by a mere Westminster majority.

The funds that we had raised were put towards the costs incurred in defending the Lords' case in both these hearings.

Our June 2000 newsletter had better news, delightedly reporting that 'Parliament Bounces Back'. Blair had axed 650 hereditary Peers, but the Lords came back fighting. They debated, and decided, on several issues which Tony was not enthusiastic about.

These issues included:

- rejecting curbs on jury trials which would reduce punishments for the guilty, while exposing the innocent to miscarriages of justice;
- upholding the rights of voters in the London Mayoral Elections to receive free mail shots from candidates;
- defending the right of local authorities to decide their own management systems;
- calling a halt to what they saw as the persecution of grammar schools. That we still have some grammar schools in the country is largely down to this vote.

We later spent some of the money we had raised on producing an informative illustrated booklet entitled 'The Work of the House of Lords' which explained very clearly what the Lords did. For the majority of people in the country who were unaware of what happened in the Lords this was extremely helpful. (As an aside, it is interesting to note that our booklet has since become something of a 'blueprint' on explaining the work of the House of Lords. The Information Office is now responsible for updating the information contained in this booklet – which they do on a regular basis – and it continues to be a source of help and guidance.)

In 2007–8 the booklet explained pre-legislative scrutiny and discussed some Bills – but only some – which had been subject to this scrutiny, including:

- the Climate Change Bill;
- the Human Fertilisation and Embryology Bill (amendments rejected were the tightening of the controls on stem cell research, insisting on father figures for IVF babies, vetoing 'saviour siblings' and removal of the right to abortion on the grounds of foetal abnormality);
- the Counter-Terrorism Bill (the House voted by a majority of 191 to reject the 42-day precharge detention proposal and the Government did not insist on reinstating it in the Commons).

No small matters…

The booklet also listed key statistics about Bills handled and received, and amendments tabled and passed. Debates on such matters as architecture, the Severn barrage, funding shortages in the Armed Forces and Post Office closures were all briefly covered. There were diagrams showing who sits where, and photographs of Members, the Chamber and the Investigative Committees (many of whose concerns remain valid today). The Communications Committee – for example – has a photograph of Alastair Campbell and the now-familiar face of Rebekah Brooks giving evidence on an inquiry into media ownership and its impact on news provision … what goes around comes around!

Meanwhile Tony Blair continued, inexorably, on his crusade. Although he had promised to create a statutory Appointments Commission to oversee future Membership of the Lords, he instead appointed an interim quango, with no timetable for its replacement. Our newsletter pointed out that he had simply swapped making appointments himself for appointing people to make appointments for him.

Blair then declared he wanted to modernise procedures in the Lords. Now remember that the Speaker in the House of Lords has less authority than his/her Commons counterpart. This is because the Lords tend to regulate themselves.

The Speaker does not call the House to order or rule on points of order, call Members to speak, or select amendments. Members are therefore required to behave with self-restraint and decency, and things have to be done by agreement. There are no timetabling motions, no guillotines to cut short debate. There are no timed votes, so issues – however difficult – can be properly addressed and thrashed out. Every Peer is equal – free to set down an amendment, ask a question, table a motion and have it debated or heard.

The most recent plan to get rid of more Members of the Lords was just as bonkers as the first one. Nick Clegg – Deputy Prime

Minister – had published a plan to replace the Lords with a wholly (or 80 per cent) elected Chamber, consisting of about 300 Peers. These Members would be elected by thirds every five years, and each would serve one fifteen-year term. However, this threatened to provoke a crisis as most Peers believed it to be unconstitutional.

In response to a *Times* newspaper questionnaire sent to all those entitled to sit in the House of Lords, some 310 responded. Of those, 80 per cent opposed the plan with 74 per cent believing it would be unconstitutional to use the Parliament Act to push it through, and 81 per cent believing that 'if it ain't broke, why fix it?'

Even Clegg's Peers were not keen on his proposal; ex-Liberal Leader, David Steel, was one of the most vociferous, stating that he believed 'An increasing number of MPs are also recognising the dangers of an elected Upper House undermining the primacy of the House of Commons.'

He also said he wanted to introduce a retirement scheme, and to establish an independent Appointments Commission for new Peers, in order to avoid any future 'cash for Peerages' scandals.

In his House of Lords Bill, Lord Steel has said:

The House is becoming irritated by being asked to consider long-term changes to an Elected Chamber, while the need to reform the present one gets neglected. I am old enough to recall that this is precisely what happened in the late '60s ... history looks as though it may repeat itself.

Lord Steel continues to be critical of these plans for the reform of the Lords and has – in recent years – introduced several

Private Members' Bills, and Baroness Hayman has now also become involved.

There was no consensus amongst Peers for reform and eventually, in 2012, the plan was dropped (ostensibly on the pretext that there was not enough time before the end of the parliamentary session to allow proper discussion of the matter).

On 28 March 2014 a group of Labour Peers put forward yet another suggestion for the reform of the Lords. It is to be hoped that sense will prevail and that this latest attempt to force change will also be thrown out.

CHAPTER TWENTY-ONE

OTHER PEOPLE'S
MEMORIES

Sir John Major

Basil was always easy to work with. I cannot recall a single cross word. He knew what needed to be done, and what he was able to do. He neither asked for – nor needed – any help, and just got on with the job.

❦

I cannot recall where I first met Basil, but I most certainly recall my first impressions. Basil struck me as a soft-spoken but totally dedicated supporter of the Party, who always did more than he promised – rather than less. I remember thinking how refreshing that was. I was also struck by the easy relationship he had with everyone around him.

Most typically I remember Basil charming groups of influential and undecided voters to become supporters, and committed supporters to become contributors. He did this by explanation and exhortation, and also by example. Basil never asked anyone to do what he had not already done, and I think this was the main reason he was so successful.

Basil was always easy to work with. I cannot recall a single cross word. He knew what needed to be done, and what he was able to do. He neither asked for – nor needed – any help, and just got on with the job. Moreover, he did it very successfully; I remember once thinking that if every Constituency had two Basils we would have no more organisational concerns whatsoever.

As a fundraiser, Basil was the complete package; persuasive, persevering and unthreatening. But Basil did much more than simply raise money for the Party. In good times and in bad he kept talking to supporters and contributors, and had a gift for making them feel wanted and needed – as, indeed, they were. Basil really was immensely valuable to the Conservative Party, and the Party should be enormously grateful for all he did.

Sir John Major, KG, CH, PC, is a Conservative politician who served as Prime Minister of the United Kingdom and Leader of the Conservative Party from 1990 to 1997. He held the posts of Foreign Secretary and Chancellor of the Exchequer in the Cabinet of Margaret Thatcher, and was the Member of Parliament for Huntingdon from 1979 to 2001. Despite the British economy then being in recession, he led the Conservatives to a fourth consecutive Election victory – winning the most votes in British electoral history in the 1992 General Election, albeit with a much reduced majority in the House of Commons. He is – to date – the last Conservative Leader to win an outright majority in a General Election.

The Lord Harris of Peckham

I like Basil because he is a doer. We speak twice a week, and always speak our minds. Ninety-eight per cent of the time, we think the same way.

❦

I first met Basil when he was working for Mrs Thatcher.

He had so much energy, so many ideas. He was a very, very hard worker; no one has worked harder than him for the Conservatives, and given up his own time and business to do so.

He is absolutely brilliant. He put Better Made in Britain on the map for our industry. It was entirely his idea, and he made it very successful.

We went into the Lords together in 1995; we've not only worked together, but we are very good friends. Also, he always gives you a sweet when you meet him there!

He's been helpful with academies. We have fourteen academies and all have been judged outstanding by Ofsted. If it wasn't for Basil, I would not have got involved. I owe him a great deal – he convinced me to do it.

We have often travelled to countries together. He was always there on Election night with me. We went round quite a few seats together and met the potential MPs, and he did it with fun. It was serious, but we enjoyed doing what we were doing together.

I was 100 per cent behind him in his efforts for the reform of the

House of Lords and, of course, backed him and raised money for it. I thought it was really important.

Thatcher thought the world of Basil. Even in later years, when she was not so well, I used to visit her four or five times a year – and I always talked to her about Basil.

I have many memories of our work and friendship over the years. I remember Basil arranging meetings with people outside business and bringing people into the Party who were never Conservative backers. He raised many millions for the Conservatives.

He has a lovely wife and they work together as a family. We often arrange dinners out together; he sits next to my wife, Pauline, and they write poems together. He says she is better than him! We think they are two of the best.

We have stayed very good friends, and I am sure that we will continue to be – I don't think we have ever had a disagreement.

The Lord Harris of Peckham established Harris Carpets in 1964, and in 1977 the company merged with Queensway to become Harris Queensway. He remained as Chairman and CEO of that company until 1988. He has been Chairman of Harris Ventures since 1988, Chairman and CEO of Carpetright since 1993, and non-Executive Director of Carpetright since July 2014. Lord Harris was Deputy Chairman of the Conservative Party Board of Treasurers from 1993 to 1997 and has also been a non-Executive Director of Arsenal Football Club since 2003. Lord Harris became a Member of the House of Lords in January 1996.

Sheila Hale MBE

He's got more energy and enthusiasm than anyone I've ever met before.

☙

One day in early 1983 an employment agency suggested that I should meet Basil, with a view to becoming his new PA. At the time he was quite high up within the Conservative Party – and I had virtually *no* experience of politics of any kind. However, I had an open mind, and so I went along for a chat.

I can't really remember what, exactly, we discussed – but after about a half an hour of general chitchat Basil said, 'So, do you want the job?' and I said, 'Yes!' And so began one of the most extraordinary periods of my life.

I can honestly say that I've never once been bored. During our time together we have worked on so many different projects. Apart from his political work – including his work to ensure the voluntary party was recognised, acknowledged and used properly, there were the pre-Election rallies (which were huge fun, and very successful), the charitable events we ran for the Conservative National Golf Tournament, various Better Made in Britain exhibitions, Sunday Trading, working to try and save the hereditary Peers, his Chairmanship of the Renaissance Forum and all the dinners we ran for that donor club, our plan for a cost-effective way to rebuild the Royal National Orthopaedic Hospital ... the list goes on.

Basil is a one-off. A true patriot who, when he has an idea, will stop at nothing to make it happen. If he feels that something is worth doing he simply won't accept 'No' for an answer – and in fact I've often joked that he's like a bulldog when he gets his teeth into something new!

The people who know him well simply adore him – as do I – not least because of his sense of loyalty and fair play.

Gita calls us a *'folie à deux'* as she says we are both as mad as each other when we get started on a new project – and all I can say to this is that I can't think of a better description of my working life with an extraordinary man.

Sheila has been at Basil's right hand for the past thirty years. She organises his office – and his life – and generally ensures that everything runs as smoothly as it possibly can.

Chris Poole CBE

You don't always remember group leaders coming to see you because there are so many – but nobody ever forgot Basil. He was a larger-than-life character, very, very enthusiastic about what he was doing.

❦

I first met Basil in February 1974, during the General Election when he brought a team of volunteers from London to help canvass and campaign for a marginal seat in Reading.

At the time, he was a Constituency Chairman in Greater London Area, moving up the ladder in volunteer politics and reasonably influential in London – but not that well known outside the capital at that time.

I will never forget him chairing one of the Party Conferences in Blackpool. I was responsible – as agents were – for stewarding a certain area of the Winter Gardens. Normally the Chairman would come from his hotel by car and go through the back entrance near the stage, so there was no hassle and no fuss, and then progress unobtrusively into the Green Room.

Not this time; all of a sudden Basil came through the main entrance. As soon as he walked through the door he went up to all the stewards, shook their hands, and said, 'Thank you for what you are doing.'

I have never seen this happen before or since, and it was a master stroke.

It didn't cost anything, and only took ten minutes or so – but it meant an awful lot to people who were on their feet every day from 8 a.m. to 6 p.m. It was typical of him, and it made an enormous impression on everyone.

He was a pleasure to work with – completely straightforward. He knew what he wanted, and made this clear, but that was fine. He was very, very fair and full of energy and enthusiasm – and he was always very concerned for other people.

I sat next to him on the platform at the Party Conference. We organised every debate and sat there from 9.30 a.m. to 5.30 p.m. Other people came and went, but the only two constants were the two of us.

Although we were under pressure all of the time it was good fun.

I remember he crunched (never sucked!) his way through a handful of boiled sweets, and would ask me to get more if I was going out at lunchtime. Eventually I wrote to one of the sweet companies, told them what we did, and said that Basil's crunching was costing me a fortune!

They sent me a five pound jar of boiled sweets which I gave to Basil one lunchtime as a present.

Some years later, when Basil finished his term as Chairman of the National Union Executive Committee, we thought long and hard about what to give him. I suggested to the Officers of the Committee that we should have a pair of porcelain bowls made in the same design as a dining set that had been commissioned by the Sultan of Oman through Royal Doulton, and which were gold and blue in colour, with a crest. We wrote to Royal Doulton and asked them if – instead of the Sultan's crest – they could put Basil's coat of arms in the middle of the bowls. The final effect was stunning and he was very pleased.

Basil loved letters – he loved writing them, and receiving them. He didn't need a reason; he would take his books to read on holidays, and when he had returned there were all sorts of notes in the margins, and then he would write letters to the authors. He is a great written communicator.

I therefore decided that as part of his leaving gift I would write to as many people I could think of who knew him, and ask them to write a letter about him which we could put together in a folder, and present him together with the bowls. I think he appreciated those letters almost more than he did the bowls!

Basil's got pulling power. He always got good speakers, and made plenty of money for Party funds. The point was to bring people back into the organisation and to make them feel that they were still involved. Then, come Election time, there was a wealth of experience at our disposal – and most people were prepared to go to marginal seats and help us campaign.

They are now old friends, who share their love of the Conservative Party.

Chris Poole CBE has a reputation as a professional organiser and Director – and in addition to being a Toastmaster and Master of Ceremonies, is also in demand as an after-dinner speaker.

Sir John Mason CBE

I found his ideas and his creative mind to be the most appealing things about the man.

❧

I have known Basil for a long time, and am a great admirer of his.

He is a man with tremendous energy, and he's got ideas. He gets irritated when people don't do what they say they are going to do, and when they don't listen. However, he is often right, and if only people had listened to him, the Conservative Party wouldn't have got itself into the mess it did.

Most importantly, Basil has never lost touch with the ordinary man. He is in tune with the vast majority of the British people, and their perceptions of the world.

We met through politics, and always had the best time.

We once went over to Berlin for two or three days, to talk to the politicians there, having been invited by the Christian Democratic Union (CDU). A few months ago he sent me a few old photos of our trip together, from which it is obvious that we were having a wonderful time. People were always relaxed with him. He has a great capacity for getting on with people and for socialising – although I don't think I have ever seen him drink alcohol. He also keeps himself tremendously fit.

A typical Basil story is the way he reacted when he heard that my wife was ill. He contacted me nearly every day to find out how she was and offered to arrange for transport to bring her down to London to be at the best possible hospital. I didn't take him up on it, but the offer meant a lot – I don't think many people know about that. Part of Basil's strength is his wife, Gita – and so he understands how important my wife is to me.

I owe a lot to Basil – he is a great and very loyal friend. When I was Vice Chairman and then Chairman of the National Union the phone would ring at 11 a.m. on most Saturday mornings. It would be Basil, and we would enjoy a good chinwag about things.

He was a damned hard-working, decent man, and I did my utmost to get him elected as Chairman of the National Union Executive Committee. I failed the first time, when he was beaten by Peter Lane, but I batted strongly – and successfully – for him. He is a man of quality.

He had tremendous ambition – both for the Party and for himself – which was absolutely fine. I would much rather a man be ambitious and say so, than pretend he wasn't. You knew just where you were with Basil.

Sir John Mason has always had an active interest in politics. He is also President of the Scunthorpe and District Choral Society, and President of the Scunthorpe and District Scouts Association. He is a passionate supporter of Scunthorpe United and Chairman of Humberside ProHelp. Sir John was actively involved in the NHS from 1978 to 2006, having been Chairman of the Scunthorpe and District Health Authority, Chairman of the Scunthorpe and Goole NHS Hospital Trust and, from 2001 to 2006, Chairman of the North Lincolnshire Primary Care Trust. He was awarded the CBE in 1989 and in 1994 had the honour of a knighthood conferred upon him. He was appointed Deputy Lord Lieutenant of Lincolnshire in 2006. Sir John passed away, after a long illness, at the end of June 2014. His wife, Maggie, continues to live in the family home in Winterton, north Lincolnshire.

Jim Hodkinson

Basil is someone who is always full of common sense – which is quite unusual.

❦

My first conversations with Basil were through Better Made in Britain (BMIB). At that time I was Chief Executive of B&Q, and I think we met at a BMIB exhibition.

Our buying director said, 'This will be a complete waste of time,' but I told him that, as we are the biggest UK DIY company, we have to support these sorts of things. And I am glad that we did.

Basil was passionate about getting more and more products made in this country, and in the end we decided that we would try to do something in our stores to help. He organised it all, and we were successful in returning manufacturing to the UK – which at that time made a hell of a difference in bringing jobs back to the UK.

If I had a particular issue that needed some political weight behind it he would be marching me down to see a particular Secretary of State or minister in a very short time.

We tried to get into the Northern Ireland market and, at the time, came across lots of obstacles. I asked for his help, and soon he had me sitting there with the Secretary of State for Northern Ireland, talking about how we could get B&Q there. Next we had a meeting with the local authority in Belfast!

He was, without doubt, instrumental in enabling B&Q to get

into Northern Ireland, and I am sure – had it not been for his help – that we would have had to wait for a very long time.

I also remember him as a wonderful fixer – bringing people together. He was Chairman of the Sunday Trading campaign which worked to change the law to enable shops to open on a Sunday.

The Sunday Trading campaign needed a heavyweight like Basil to get it all moving – and he succeeded.

I have known him for a long time, and we still have lunch together a couple of times a year. I know I can call on him at any time and ask for help and advice.

He has been a good friend to me; he always has words of encouragement, no matter when, and I am delighted that we still keep in touch.

Jim Hodkinson served as Chairman and Chief Executive of B&Q plc (a subsidiary of Kingfisher plc) from 1995 to 1998. Mr Hodkinson served as Chief Executive of New Look plc from 1998 to May 2000. He started his career at F. W. Woolworth Limited in 1962 as a Trainee Manager. He joined B&Q in 1972, and served as its Operations Director from 1979 and Group Managing Director from 1986.

David Ramsden

One of the most striking things about Basil is his great generosity.

❦

Basil is a charming chap, very energetic. One of his strengths is the people he knows, and the people he can persuade. He's never backward in coming forward if he can see that there is something he might be able to do.

Basil is never deliberately rude to anyone. He is also a generous host and always provided lunch when we used to go to his office for meetings.

I am always amused at the memory I have of those days – we would sit down to eat, and he would always swivel his tie round to the back of his neck before he got started. He never got any food down his tie!

We worked together on the Sunday Trading campaign. Before that, I had been Head of Public Affairs at Kingfisher, and I joined the Shopping Hours Reform Council as their Deputy Director.

It was incredibly hard work, and Basil did all he could to generate support – hosting dinners at the Carlton Club, attending our weekly management meetings and doing his best to encourage the Party to get behind our campaign.

I have now retired, but even so, I will periodically get a telephone call – 'It's Basil, how are you doing, boy?' – and we have a chat. We also always get a card from him and his wife at Christmas.

He is truly a very good friend.

David Ramsden was formerly Head of Public Affairs at Kingfisher plc before becoming Deputy Director of the Shopping Hours Reform Council in 1984 where he remained for several years. Later, in 1994, he once again chaired a lobby group called Deregulate which worked to amend the Sunday Trading hours.

Roger Boaden OBE

He demanded much – but gave even more.

☙

For two decades of my political and working life Basil Feldman was a dominant character. He was head and shoulders more influential than anyone else in my life.

Basil had fought a hard campaign to become a member of the GLC.

Although he failed, after taking time to analyse his defeat he discovered that the Party had next to nothing in the way of campaigning literature or manuals, and any enquiry he made for such things had often been met with blank stares.

He therefore decided to design his own campaigning booklet. I was exhilarated by the infectious drive and vigour he displayed in presenting this idea – and also impressed that he was prepared to put his money where his mouth was.

When the decision was made to go ahead and write the booklet, Basil pressed for me to be allowed to work with him on it. This incredible loyalty is typical of the man.

We spoke most days, and lunched at least once a week until the project was complete, and I found that – despite the pressures on him – he always had time for me.

He was always prepared to roll up his sleeves and work alongside anyone to achieve success for the Party, and he won myriad supporters at grass roots level.

We eventually published *Constituency Campaigning – a guide for all Party workers* in January 1977, and it achieved widespread praise and support, particularly from many of my professional agent colleagues who had long cried out for something simple and yet comprehensive.

With his usual panache, Basil persuaded Mrs Thatcher to help launch the publication, and this gave it a much wider audience than might otherwise have been achieved.

Basil was always smartly dressed from head to toe. His long hair and – in the early days – long sideburns, his tight trousers, with a hanky in the top pocket of his jacket gave him an almost dandyish appearance. What this did was to make him stand out from the crowd; he was different, and he looked different from the many time servers – often drab, colourless people – that he came up against.

He taught me how to network, and I admired the way in which he could sweep into a gathering, seek out his immediate targets, and – having completed his exchanges – start all over again seeking a new set of targets. He knew exactly how to work a room.

Over the next decade I met Mrs Thatcher on numerous occasions, and I recall frequent mentions of 'Dear Basil'. He maintained his contact with her, counselled her and offered his advice – and always with the greatest of charm.

Basil's regular contacts with her were very helpful and important to him during his progress to the top of the National Union, as Chairman of the National Union Executive Committee – a position he held from 1991 to 1996. I'm as sure as I can be that he was a million miles away from the sycophants who surrounded her in those days, as he was one of those who were always completely open and honest with her at all times.

Roger Boaden worked for many years within the Conservative Party – before moving on to take on a new role as Campaign Director of the Shopping Hours Reform Campaign. He now lives in France and has become a published author.

CHAPTER TWENTY-TWO

TOWARDS THE FUTURE

Many people ask me what I'm doing these days, and the answer is: much the same as I always did – although perhaps not quite as much of it!

The truth is that I can't believe I have reached the great age of ninety. The years have gone by so fast, and there is still so much I want to do.

I believe in keeping active and interested in all things. I still come into the office four days a week and I occasionally attend the Lords when it is in session (more so if we have a particularly important vote).

I maintain my interest in theatre, opera and, of course, football; I watch Arsenal, as always, with my two sons, whenever they play at home. Gita and I continue to visit Salzburg each August for the summer music festival and we go to the National Theatre and the Royal Opera House as often as we can.

My family continues to be a source of great joy and comfort to me. All of the grandchildren are grown now and pursuing their careers. They have all turned out to be wonderful, warm and caring people, and I am extremely proud of them.

Gita and I celebrated our sixtieth wedding anniversary last October, with lunch at the Savoy. We have used this hotel for our special anniversaries ever since we got married (when we spent our first few nights as newlyweds there, before we travelled out to the United States).

Cutting the cake at our sixtieth anniversary

We also recently held a family lunch there to celebrate my nineti-eth birthday, and I hope we shall continue to celebrate important family occasions at the hotel in the years ahead.

With Gita, for my ninetieth party at the Savoy Hotel, September 2013

As part of my ninetieth birthday celebrations, my former colleagues from within the National Union organised a lunch at the Carlton Club. Brian Hanson told me that, when he was compiling the guest list, he had decided to invite people who had all held the position of Conference Chairman, and with whom I had worked during my days as National Union Chairman.

It was wonderful to have an opportunity to talk to so many old friends; I felt young once more, reminded of our work together, and all the things we had achieved within the Party.

My one sadness, on the day, was that a dear friend – John Mason – was unable to be there as he was critically ill. He was, however, in our thoughts and we raised a glass to him during the lunch.

I intend to carry on working for as long as I am able to do so, because I do believe it is important as one ages to keep mind and body active. I want to continue to make a contribution to the community, and to a country that I believe to be the best in the world. I don't know how long I will be able to do this, but I continue to enjoy my life and hope that I will do so for a long while to come!

ACKNOWLEDGEMENTS

First, and foremost, I want to thank my wife, Gita, for her love and support in everything I've done. She has been the mainstay of my life and I truly could not have achieved the things I've been able to do had it not been for her encouragement.

Thanks, also, to my children and grandchildren – of whom I am very proud. I hope this book will give them an insight into the many things that I've done – and perhaps explain why I've always been so busy!

There are too many friends and colleagues that I want to thank for their support over the years – but in particular I want to give a special thank you to Phil Harris for his unwavering friendship and good advice, which I value more than I can say.

I want to thank Sylvia Howe for helping to tease the memories from me when we first embarked on this project, and for enabling me to put them down in some sort of order.

And last – but definitely not least – I want to thank my PA, Sheila Hale, for all she has done to keep me going, and for helping me attain – and share in – the goals I have set myself over the past thirty years. I also want to particularly acknowledge her hard work in the past two years while we have been putting this book together, for helping to write, re-write, edit and proofread the chapters of my story – and for doing it all with patience and a smile.

INDEX

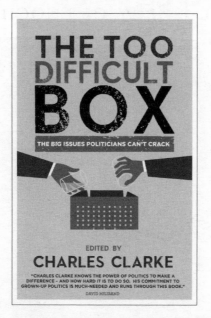

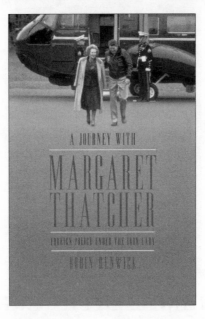